BATMAN v SUPERMAN
DAWN OF JUSTICE

TECH MANUAL

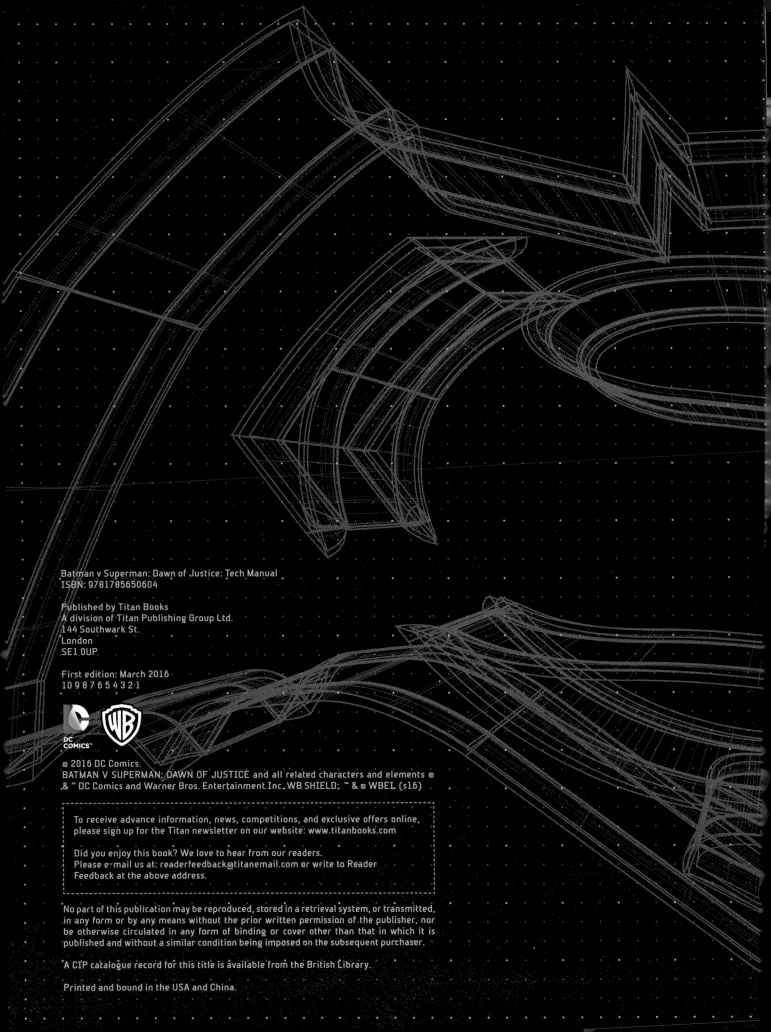

Batman v Superman: Dawn of Justice: Tech Manual
ISBN: 9781785650604

Published by Titan Books
A division of Titan Publishing Group Ltd.
144 Southwark St.
London
SE1 0UP.

First edition: March 2016
10 9 8 7 6 5 4 3 2 1

To receive advance information, news, competitions, and exclusive offers online,
please sign up for the Titan newsletter on our website: www.titanbooks.com

Did you enjoy this book? We love to hear from our readers.
Please e-mail us at: readerfeedback@titanemail.com or write to Reader
Feedback at the above address.

BATMAN v SUPERMAN
DAWN OF JUSTICE

TECH MANUAL

ADAM NEWELL & SHARON GOSLING

FOREWORD BY PATRICK TATOPOULOS

TITAN BOOKS

CONTENTS

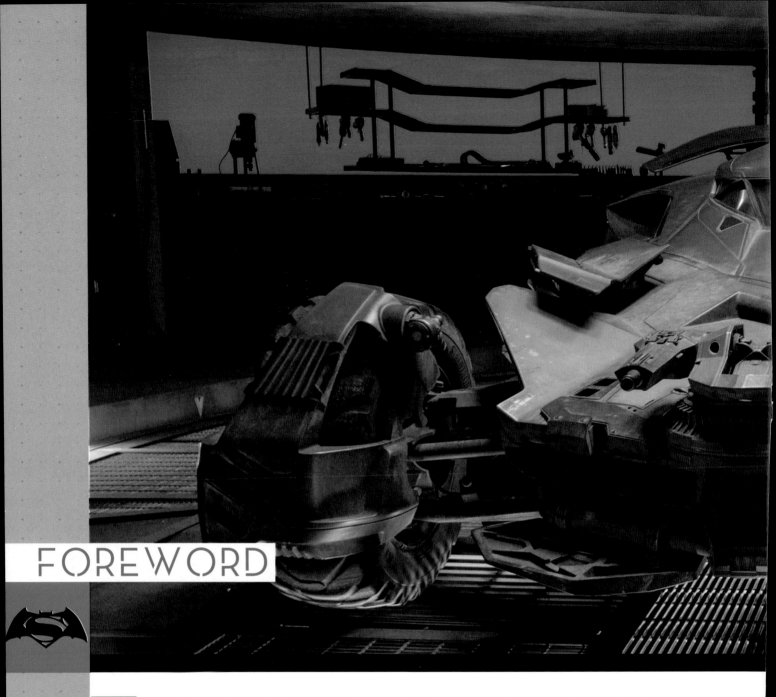

FOREWORD

When Zack Snyder reached out to me at the end of *300 Rise of An Empire* and offered me the opportunity to design his next movie, *Batman v Superman: Dawn of Justice*, I became incredibly excited. Understandably, this was a childhood dream of mine. Nonetheless, my immediate question was, is this going to be *Man of Steel* v *Dark Knight*? Two worlds already visually established. His answer was, "this is *Man of Steel*, yes - but as for Batman, it is going to be 'our Batman'". A new Batman, with a new Batmobile, a new Batcave, and a whole new world of technology.

I had hoped to work with Zack since I saw *Dawn of The Dead*, and even more so after *300*. Now he offers me a chance to create the world for his Batman. I was so excited

that after our meeting I stopped at a coffee shop on my way home, and started to design the Batmobile. For any designer working in this industry, there are just a few iconic subjects that are above anything else. Batman's world and his technology are at the top of that list. After designing the Batmobile, and getting positive feedback from Zack, I knew we had found the aesthetic and the technology for our Batman.

It always starts with one object. This is my process. It could be a single prop, a vehicle, a set—it doesn't matter. What counts is the ability to define a single character in one encompassing object. The technology and the design aesthetic for *Batman v Superman: Dawn of Justice* was driven by a few words Zack exchanged with me. This

Batman had to be tougher, bigger, and more "rugged", but also very real. I had a direction to go by. These few words, and the initial design for the Batmobile were enough to ignite the tone for the rest of the project.

Superman's technology and the world of Krypton had already been established as Zack's vision in *Man of Steel*, however, that technology is revealed to us in *Batman v Superman* as a deconstructed version in the crashed Kryptonian scout ship. We had to pull its skin off to reveal its guts, fundamentally take an established technology and reveal its inner mechanism. Regardless, I knew we had to focus on Batman first, as we had the task of creating an entire new world for his character. Additionally, we had the challenge of establishing the characters of Lex Luthor and Wonder Woman through their respective worlds and technologies. Creating multiple visual and technological facets for such cult characters, it ultimately comes down to visual balance. Starting with one key character, and then creating a cohesive look with the other components of the film. When the aesthetic for our Batman was set, I knew the rest of the design would flow around this iconic character. I could now move forward with my team and create the bulk of the *Batman v Superman* production design.

Thank you, Zack, for the opportunity of a lifetime.

PATRICK TATOPOULOS
PRODUCTION DESIGNER

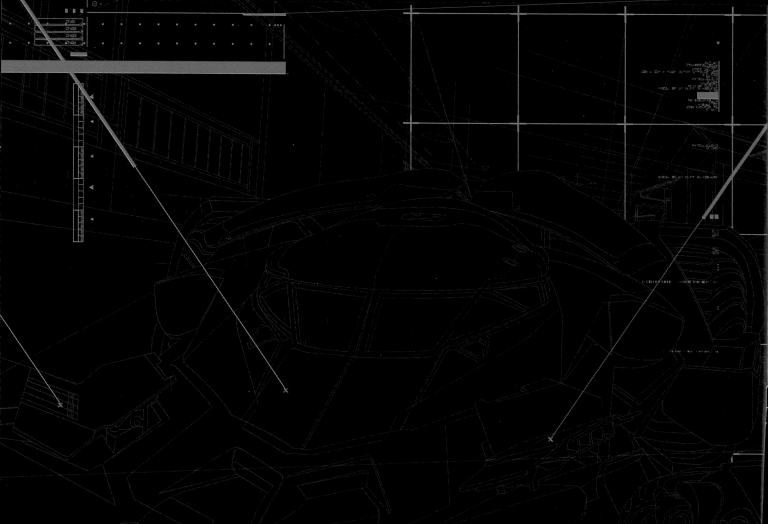

"It was amazing," says director Zack Snyder. "Suddenly, you saw the thing that you had drawn come to life." It began with the director's own early storyboards and a back-of-a-napkin sketch by production designer Patrick Tatopoulos. The Batmobile had finally become, thanks to a talented team of designers, fabricators and mechanics, a very real 20-foot long vehicle weighing 7000 lbs, with a roaring V8 engine and front-mounted twin .50 caliber machine guns.

Introducing Batman – and his arsenal of weapons and vehicles – into the world established by *Man of Steel* (2013) was an early decision in the planning stages of the follow-up film. "We'd seen Batman and Superman in comics together, but never on the big screen," says producer Deborah Snyder. "So how powerful would it be to have those two big characters together for the first time? And, of course everyone wants to see Batman and Superman fight, so we couldn't disappoint in that respect."

"They're actually opposite sides of the same coin," Zack Snyder points out. "It's interesting because Batman's a man and Superman's a god, if you think about it in those terms. So their relationship is very contentious. What Superman sees as Batman's limits, Batman sees as Superman trying to control him, acting like an absolute dictator. What we went after was the humanity of each character. We tried to say, 'What would Batman have to do to unravel Superman, and what would Superman have to do to unravel Batman?' Their conflict is based on each other's understanding of the other's weakness.

"To me it's about the drama. Those are like Shakespearean characters, Bruce Wayne and Clark Kent, they have inherent drama built into their makeup," the director continues, emphasizing the core of the film's narrative. "It's about

human stories, it's not just about big explosions. What are these people feeling?"

"Our goal from the very beginning has been to take these wonderful icons and imbue them with today's real-life issues," adds producer Charles Roven. "We thought that was a really compelling thing to do. We could make it big, a spectacle, but still make it real and make the interactions between the characters very personal, very relatable, and still have a lot of fun doing it."

This 'real world, real consequences' approach appealed to the actor chosen to embody Zack Snyder's vision, as developed in the script by David S. Goyer and Chris Terrio, of an older, seasoned Batman: Ben Affleck. "This is really taking a more nuanced view at how these types of characters may exist in the real world and what sorts of complications it might create," says Affleck. "There are some really interesting ideas, [like] Metropolis being a big, successful city, and Gotham City being a place where a lot more downtrodden people live. The whole idea of wealth and power, and the way power engenders fear. There were a lot of ideas the movie was trafficking in that made it feel real to me, and smart, so I was even more proud to be part of it."

"Our films have always been very reality based," says Deborah Snyder. "You have these magnificent godlike characters who do incredible things, but they're in our

world." Like *Man of Steel* before it, this commitment to reality is a central element of the whole visual and design aesthetic of *Batman v Superman: Dawn of Justice*. "It's why we shot most of the film on location in Michigan," Snyder continues. "We did a lot of the locations for Gotham City in downtown Detroit, and there's something authentic about the patina of the city and these buildings that have been there for a long time. The reality of these locations is hard to match by building a set. There's just something inherent in the DNA."

The Batmobile chase action sequence was a case in point: "It's really important that we have [real] locations and cars that work; that everything isn't just this [CG] virtual world," says Deborah Snyder. "The key is keeping it grounded. We shot this practically as much as we could, down to the explosions, to the car flips. There's something really exciting about that. And then when we needed to, we enhanced it with CG, [but] those moments you can't tell what's real and what's CG, that's when it's most exciting and most effective."

Costume designer Michael Wilkinson certainly had his work cut out: in addition to refining the look of the suit worn by Henry Cavill as Superman, there were various Batsuits to create from scratch, and a costume for another iconic character who would be joining the fray: Wonder Woman, as portrayed by Gal Gadot.

"There's nothing I like more than a challenge," Wilkinson admits. "I love to get outside my comfort zone and go to new creative places. Designing the costumes for *Batman v Superman* really allowed me to do this. It was an incredible 18-month experience with a costume department that at times swelled to 75 people. It is rare to have the opportunity to explore the visual world of a film in such depth, and I was accompanied on this journey by the world's best costume experts. It's a chapter of my life that I will never forget.

"I really did my homework," Wilkinson continues, detailing his preparation. "I immersed myself in the long histories of these iconic characters. I studied how they have been portrayed over the last 75 years on film, on TV, in comic books, graphic novels and video games. I studied what they mean to people, what they stand for, why they are important. I started an exhaustive search for new materials and technologies – original ways of portraying these characters that would be unlike anything audiences have seen before. I wanted the costumes to help make the characters inspirational and relevant to modern audiences."

Wilkinson could count on the support of his director: "Zack was there at every step of the way – initial meetings, concept design, prototyping, fittings, camera tests. His energy and passion were phenomenal. It was the fifth film that we have done together, so by now we pretty much finish each other's sentences!"

"When Zack called me to work with him on this, I was over the moon," remembers production designer Patrick Tatopoulos. "Which designer doesn't want to design the Batmobile and the Batcave?" After an initial discussion with the director, Tatopoulos started sketching, sparking the creation of a tough, bold new look for Batman's vehicles, tech,

and their surroundings. "I come from the world of concept art," he says. "I started as an illustrator many years ago, so for me I can't do production design on a movie without sketching things myself first. Now because these movies are very big and there's a lot of things to do, I usually try to stick to concept sketches first and then work with a larger team of people to give life to those ideas."

Concept artist Ed Natividad, a member of that team, points out that Tatopoulos's approach is different to the 'mood boards' of found images that often kick off production design ideas on films: "Unlike other shows, on this one, the good thing about working with Patrick is that he never showed me an image from a magazine. It was all something he drew, which I think reinforces that it's original and very specific."

For Tatopoulos though, "the magic comes beyond what you created. It comes with all the people working together and bringing the package together. This is where everything becomes so alive. I have been working on this movie altogether close to two years. I've never done anything like that. But the results will prove that it was worth it. Visually speaking, it's the richest movie I've ever worked on. It was the hardest project ever, and the most rewarding of all."

What's especially rewarding, for the entire design team on the film, is that *Batman v Superman: Dawn of Justice* is further establishing a world that viewers will be seeing again. As Zack Snyder gleefully admits, the film "has an eye toward the future – it's going toward Justice League. Early on, once we decided that we were going to put Batman in the movie, I was like, 'OK, good! Because you know what that means? It means the floodgates can open!'"

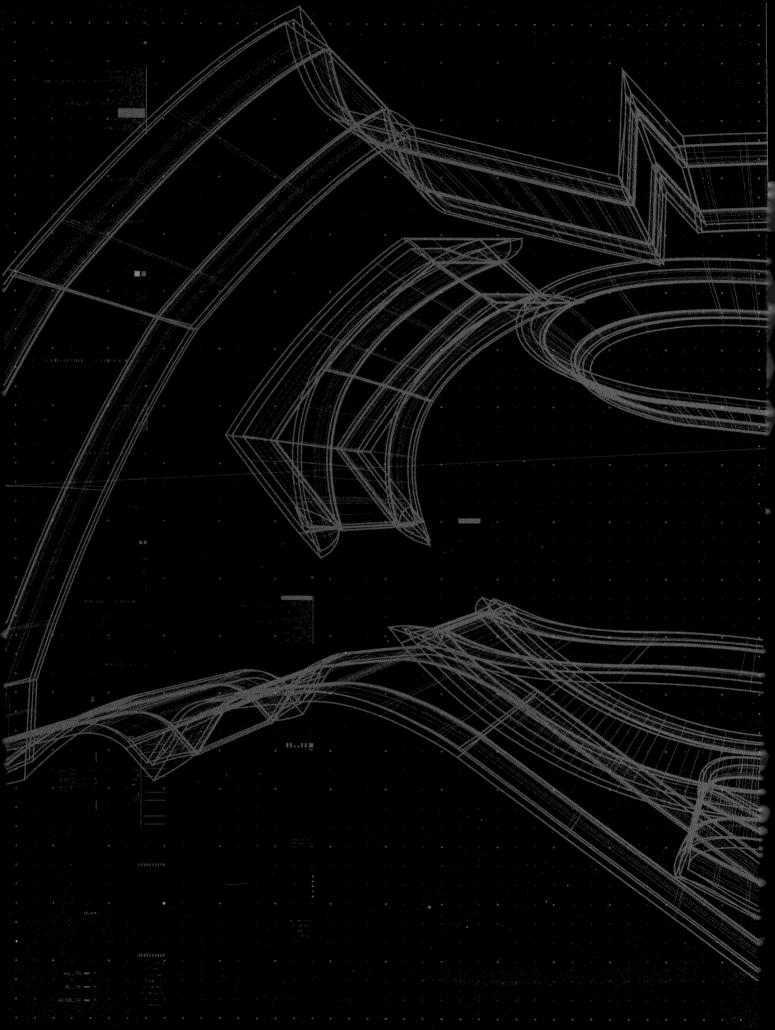

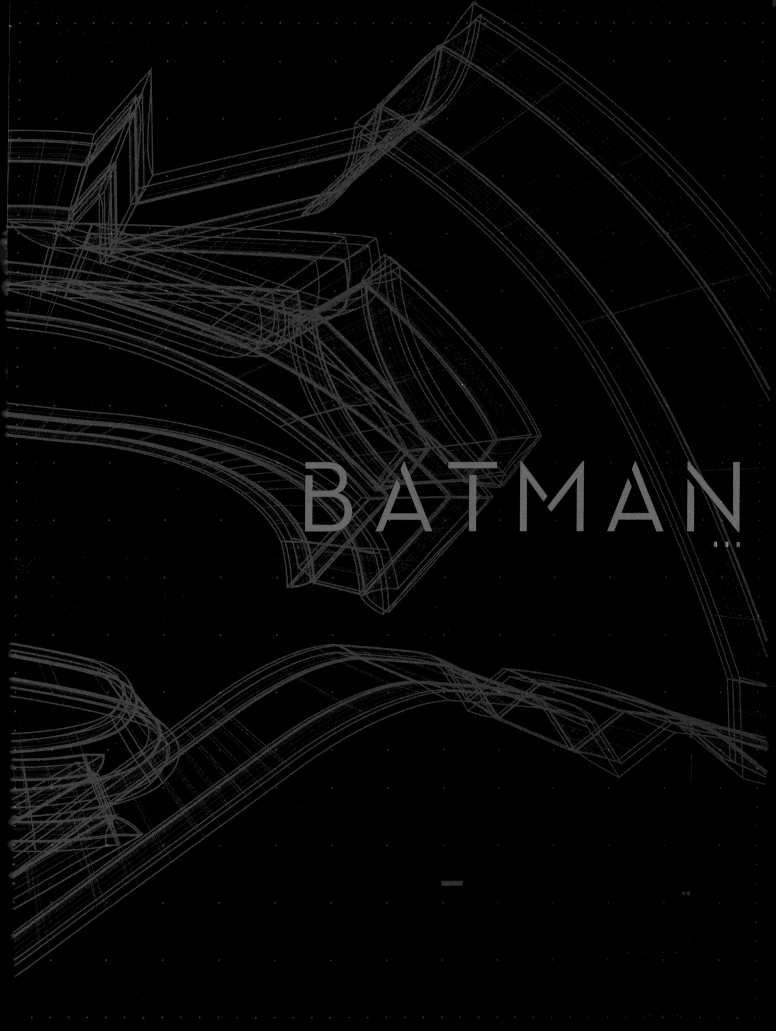

THE BATSUIT

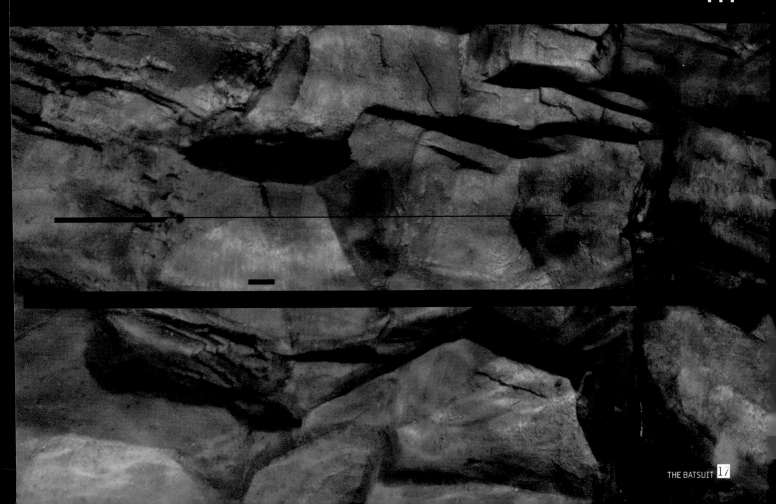

THE BATSUIT ▓ BODY ARMOR

BODY ARMOR

"My Batman is late 40s, and war weary," explains Zack Snyder. "He's been fighting crime for quite a while. He's seen it all come and go through Gotham, he's seen his family and friends come and go, live and die. He and Alfred are all that remains. He does have psychological baggage that's pretty intense and needs to be dealt with. But at the same time he's still an incredible martial artist and an incredible crime fighter, he has a great sense of right and wrong. He's dispensing vigilante justice as Batman is inclined to do. And along with that he's a genius, the greatest detective in the world and is able to manufacture and create amazing tech."

For Snyder, the design of the Batsuit was a chance to help define his vision of the character: "I wanted to make a suit that was true to the comic books and true to my take, my impression of Batman – muscular, large. That was really the genesis for the suit – make it look like it was made of fabric, even if it looked like some kind of space-age polymer. But the truth is I really just wanted it to look like a suit a man could wear, not a guy who was padded up."

It was important for Snyder that the audience look at the suit and feel that the man beneath was being defined, but not enhanced. It was a concept that costume designer Michael Wilkinson understood completely. "Zack wanted the impression that his power wasn't through the armor and the technical details of the suit, but just the brute strength of the

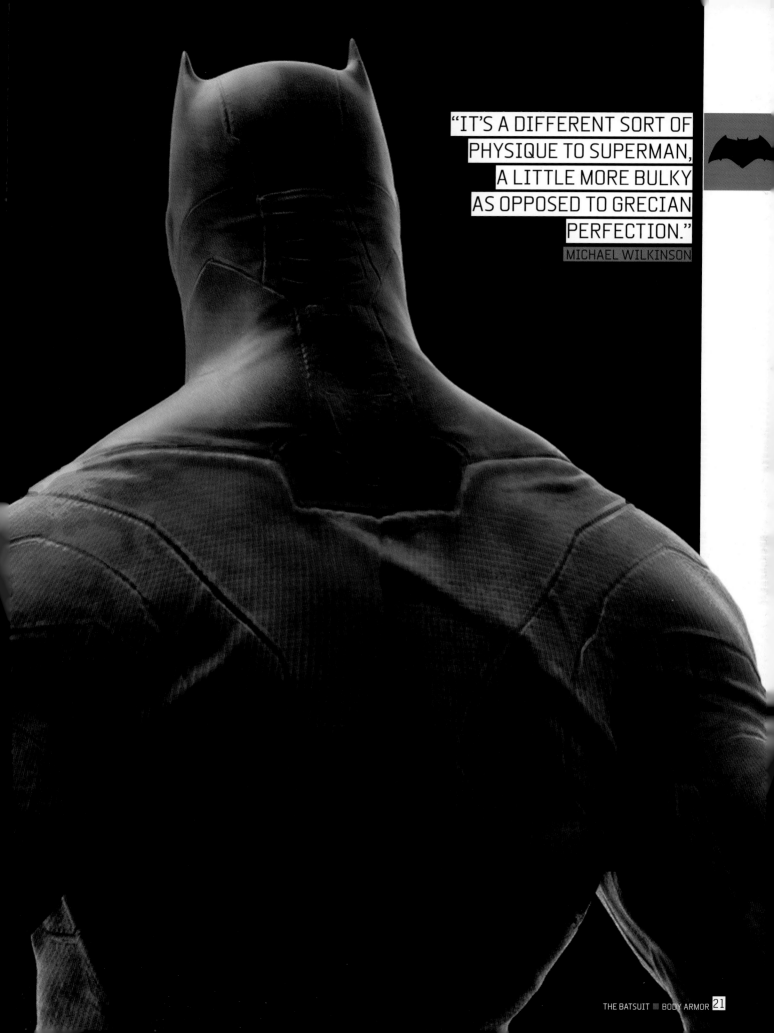

"IT'S A DIFFERENT SORT OF PHYSIQUE TO SUPERMAN, A LITTLE MORE BULKY AS OPPOSED TO GRECIAN PERFECTION."
MICHAEL WILKINSON

"FROM HEAD TO TOE, THERE'S TEXTURE EVERYWHERE – THERE'S WEAR AND TEAR."

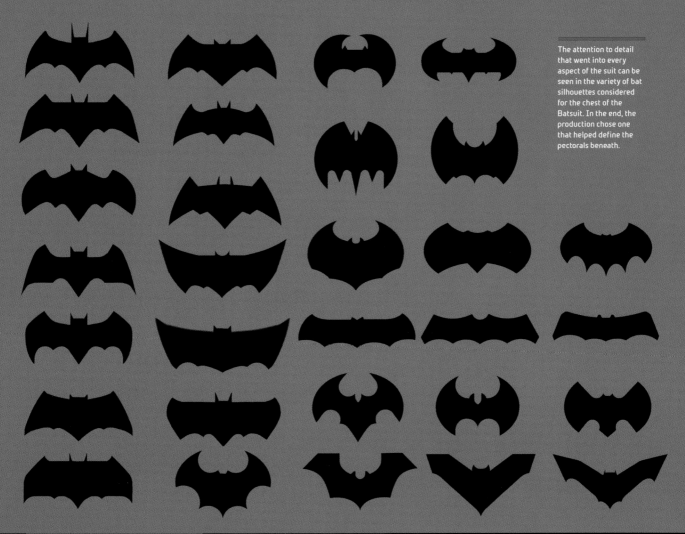

The attention to detail that went into every aspect of the suit can be seen in the variety of bat silhouettes considered for the chest of the Batsuit. In the end, the production chose one that helped define the pectorals beneath.

"The suit itself is really quite simple," says Wilkinson. "It's a thin layer of fabric that looks like a technical carbon fiber tri-weave. But it skims the body so you can see every muscle. So it's this incredibly intimidating figure that looks a lot like the way he's drawn in the graphic novel[s]. Also, Zack really wanted the costume to look like it had been around for a long time, that he'd fought in it over the decades. He wanted the sense that there is a battle-worn quality to the costume."

THE COWL

"I really wanted a one-piece cowl," explains Snyder, of the Batsuit's signature headpiece. "In the past it's been difficult for the actors who play Batman to turn their head, because of the way the cowl is connected to the piece that lays across the shoulders. So that's really the innovation – we were able to create this really thin membrane that allows the actor to look around."

Creating a one-piece cowl wasn't easy. "It's interesting," says Wilkinson. "The Batsuit may at first appearances seem quite simple and low tech, which is something that Zack had requested. But the costume technologies and the thinking that goes into achieving that look are actually pretty cutting edge." Wilkinson's team started by using the initial full-body scan they had taken of Ben Affleck to create a physical mannequin of the actor. Then Jose Fernandez of Ironhead Studio sculpted the cowl in clay over the contours of the actor's head and shoulders in order that the finished piece would be comfortable and match the wearer's actual anatomy. This sculpt was scanned back into the computer. "Then, once you have the 3D drawing, you have to make the molds, the positives and the negatives, pour the foam latex, tint the latex and paint the cowl," says Wilkinson. "It's a huge achievement in costume engineering."

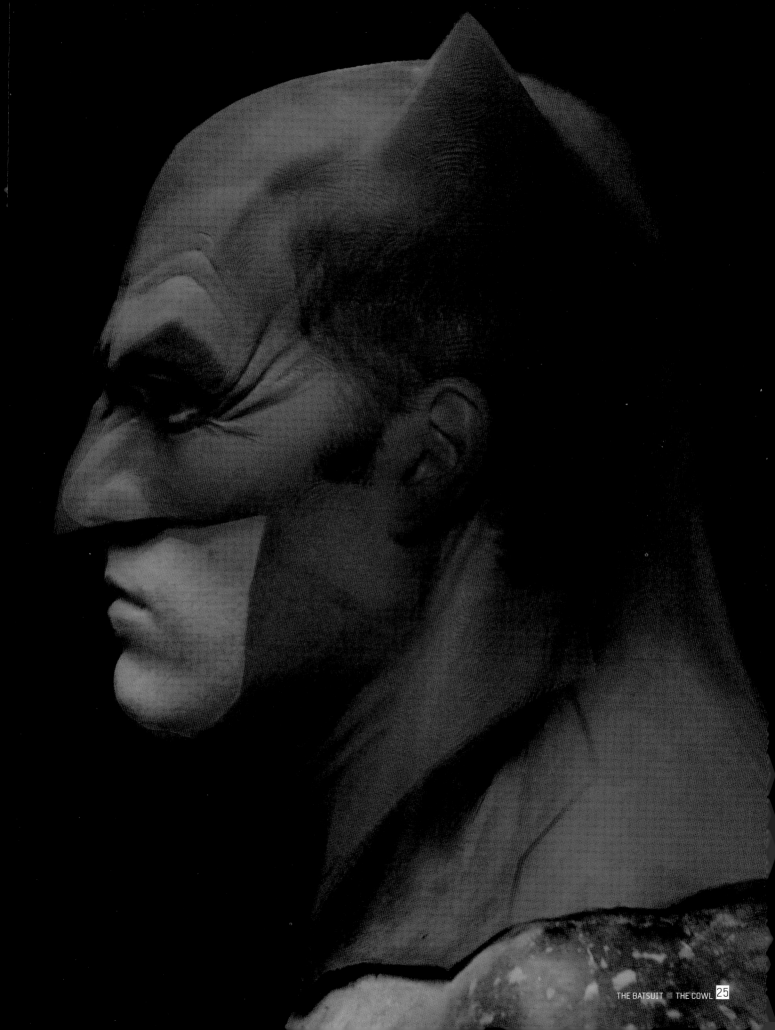

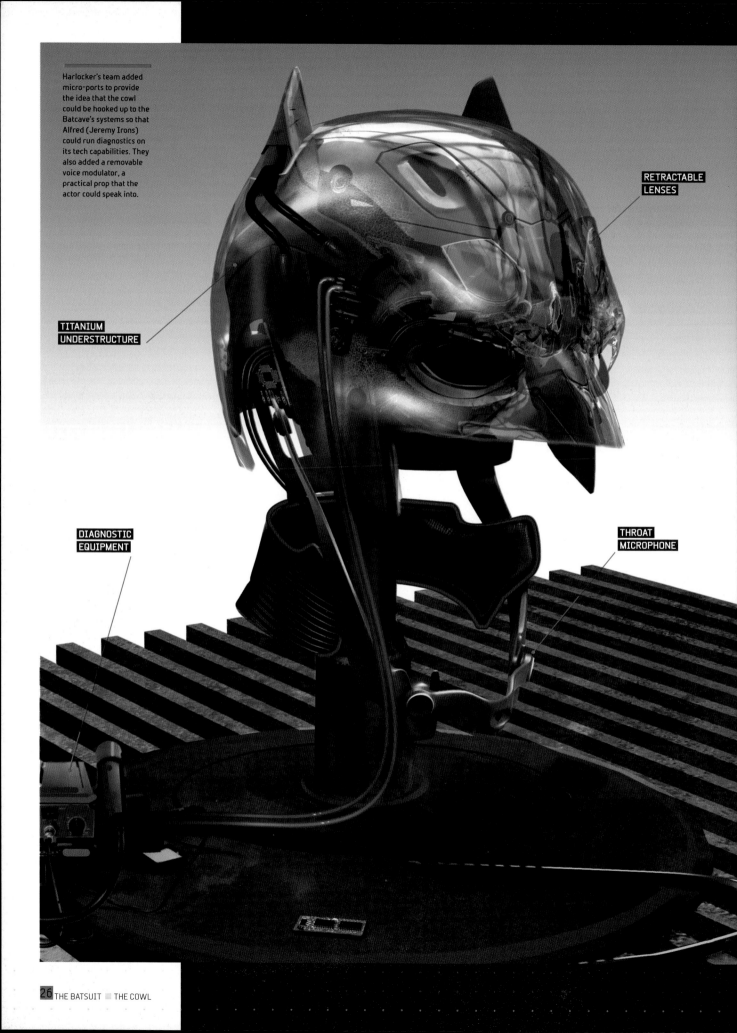

Harlocker's team added micro-ports to provide the idea that the cowl could be hooked up to the Batcave's systems so that Alfred (Jeremy Irons) could run diagnostics on its tech capabilities. They also added a removable voice modulator, a practical prop that the actor could speak into.

RETRACTABLE LENSES

TITANIUM UNDERSTRUCTURE

DIAGNOSTIC EQUIPMENT

THROAT MICROPHONE

"Zack needed something for Alfred to be working on during a discussion with Bruce in the Batcave," explains prop master Doug Harlocker. This was seen as an opportunity to show that the fabric upper of the cowl hid a protective helmet that doubled as housing for magnification and communications kits. "Of course the cowl isn't just a piece of clothing that he's wearing over his head, it's actually a huge piece of technology," says Harlocker. "We did a 3D model of it and scaled it to the outer cowl. We reverse-engineered it, we grew and molded parts and we milled certain parts out of aluminum."

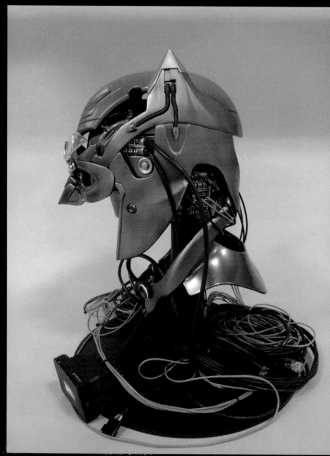

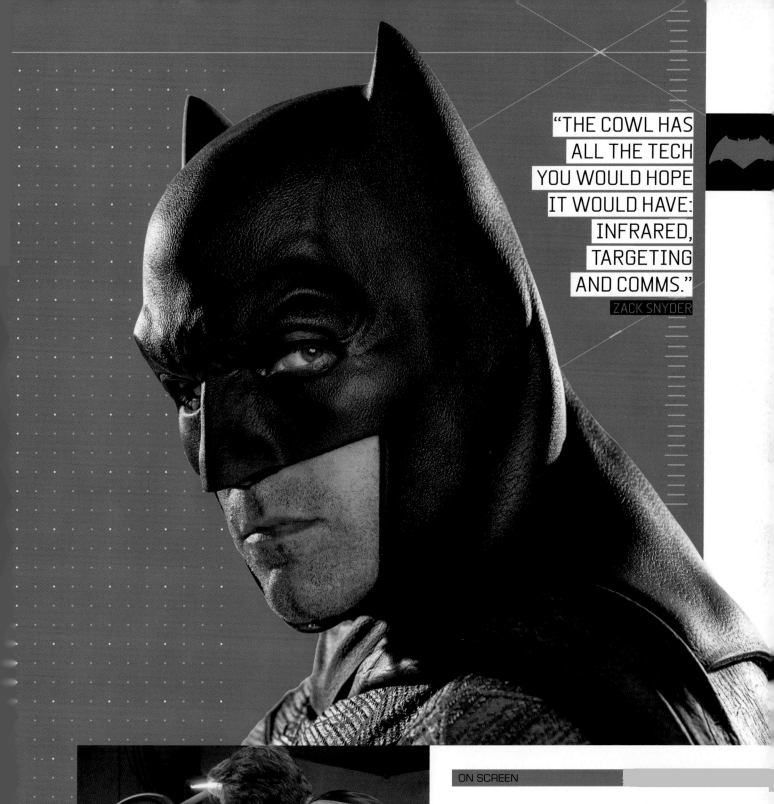

> "THE COWL HAS ALL THE TECH YOU WOULD HOPE IT WOULD HAVE: INFRARED, TARGETING AND COMMS."
>
> ZACK SNYDER

ON SCREEN

The outer costume cowl and the inner prop cowl combined on screen to create the most cohesive account of Batman's full-head mask yet seen, one that was also designed to work perfectly for what the director wanted to film. "For the first time we have a Batcowl that is comfortable and has a full range of movements," observes Wilkinson.

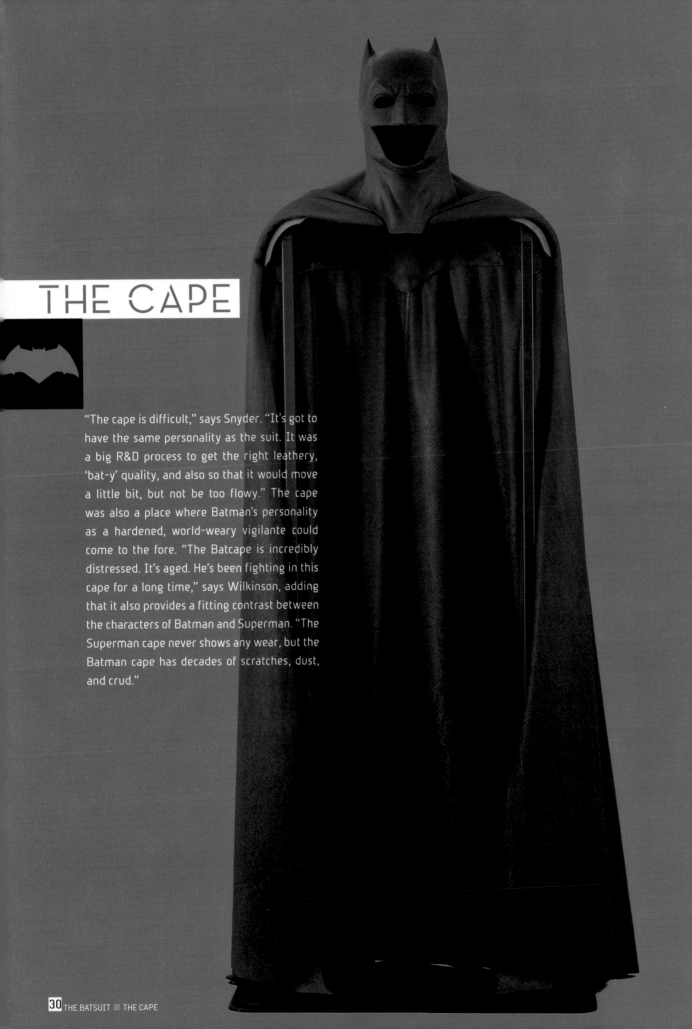

THE CAPE

"The cape is difficult," says Snyder. "It's got to have the same personality as the suit. It was a big R&D process to get the right leathery, 'bat-y' quality, and also so that it would move a little bit, but not be too flowy." The cape was also a place where Batman's personality as a hardened, world-weary vigilante could come to the fore. "The Batcape is incredibly distressed. It's aged. He's been fighting in this cape for a long time," says Wilkinson, adding that it also provides a fitting contrast between the characters of Batman and Superman. "The Superman cape never shows any wear, but the Batman cape has decades of scratches, dust, and crud."

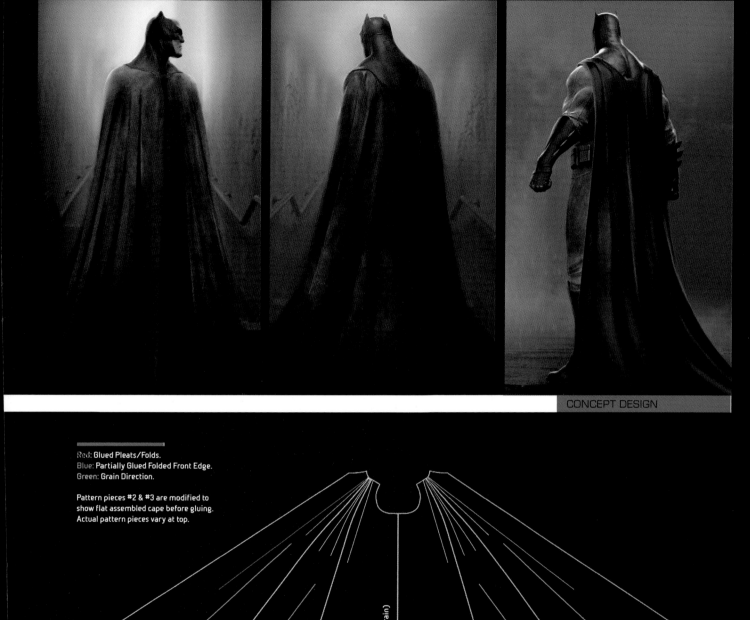

Red: Glued Pleats/Folds.
Blue: Partially Glued Folded Front Edge.
Green: Grain Direction.

Pattern pieces #2 & #3 are modified to
show flat assembled cape before gluing.
Actual pattern pieces vary at top.

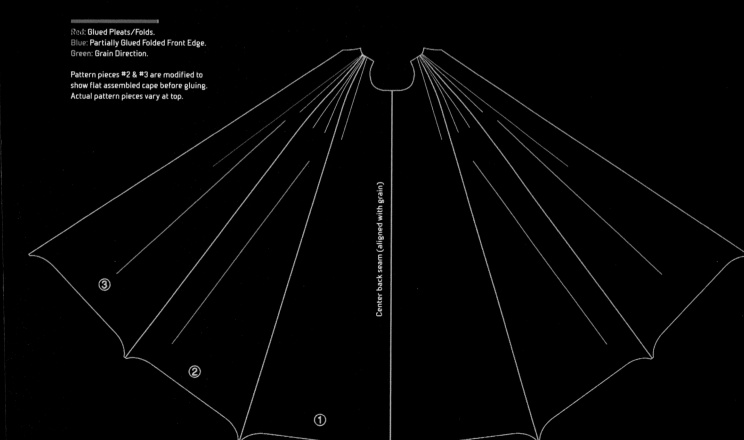

③

②

Center back seam (aligned with grain)

①

A major part of the research and development that went into the cape involved the very fabric it was made from. The costume department couldn't source a material that behaved the way they wanted it to, so there was only one solution. "The Batcape is something that we created from scratch," says Michael Wilkinson. "We created the textile. It involved pouring latex onto these amazing cape boards, laminating another fabric and then creating a digital print of the distress. So it has this really layered, encrusted feel."

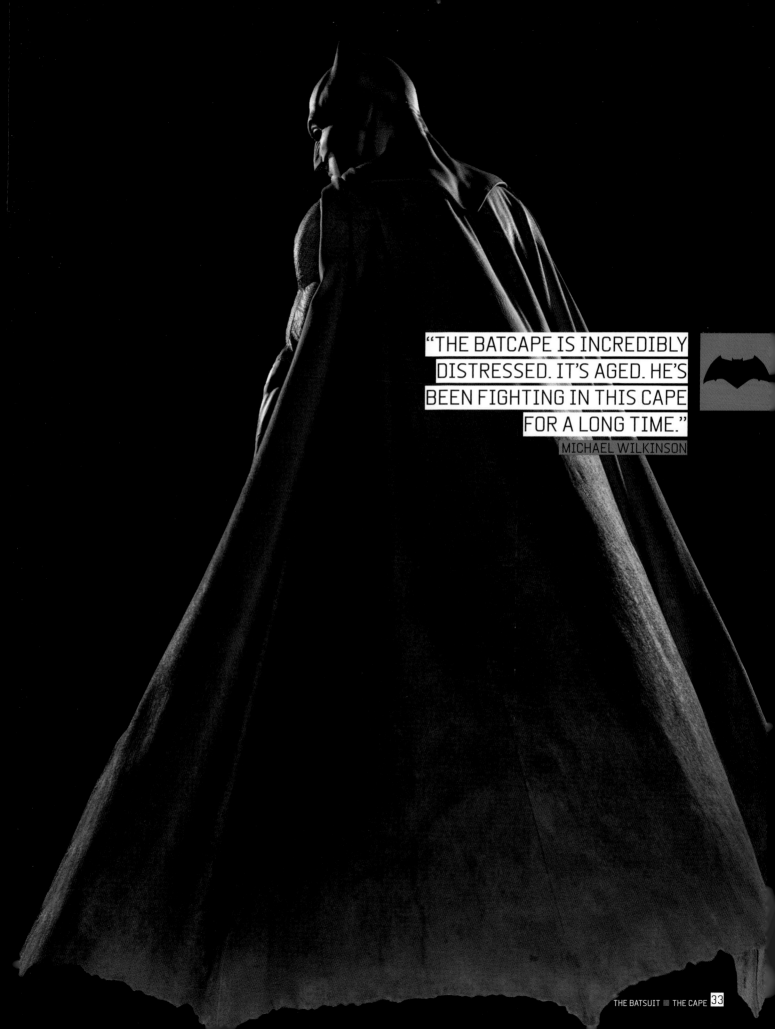

"THE BATCAPE IS INCREDIBLY DISTRESSED. IT'S AGED. HE'S BEEN FIGHTING IN THIS CAPE FOR A LONG TIME."

MICHAEL WILKINSON

UTILITY BELT

"IN HIS UTILITY BELT
BATMAN KEEPS ALL
SORTS OF INCENDIARY
AND TRACKING DEVICES,
UNDERWATER BREATHERS,
GAS MASKS, CABLES,
UNBREAKABLE WIRES –
ALL THESE KIND OF
MICRO-TOOLS."
ZACK SNYDER

From a production point of view, an item such as the Utility Belt is a close collaboration between the costume and props departments – costumes makes the belt itself and props makes everything that goes inside it. The evolution and appearance of Batman's Utility Belt in *Batman v Superman: Dawn of Justice* quietly serves as a reinforcement of the wider character of this Batman. He's not about flashy gadgets. Sure, he has them, but everything is about serving his cause, not about how it looks. So it is with the belt. He's hiding plenty of clever items in there, but he's not fussy about them. They need to be readily available, hence the boxy, one-size-fits-all nature of the holders on the belt. "One of the things that we decided early on was that we weren't going to try to define a holster and a pouch for every thing for under his cape," says prop master Doug Harlocker.

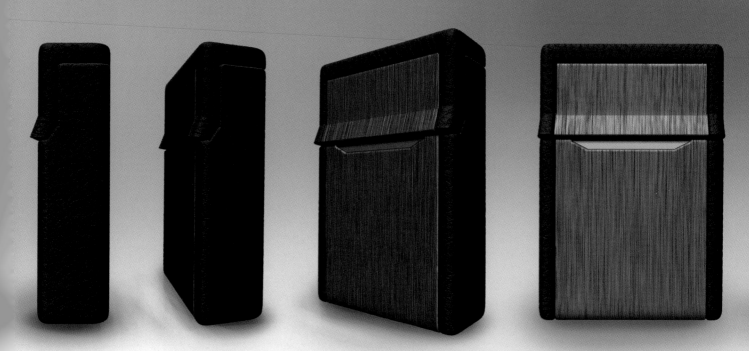

GAUNTLETS

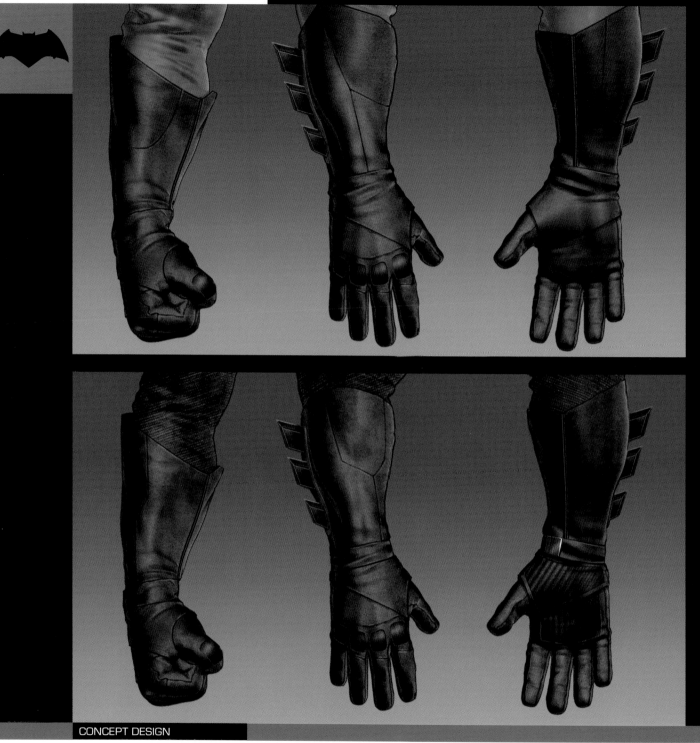

"We wanted to have him be a brawler, but also a martial artist," says Zack Snyder. "He has brute strength – kicking, striking – but he's also versed in his additional armaments, whether it be his helmet, under the cowl, the armor at his knuckles or the blades on his forearms. All of those he's incorporated into his fighting style."

Costume designer Michael Wilkinson wanted to make sure that the definition that typified the rest of the Batsuit was present even in Batman's extremities. So he made sure that the tooling and stitching of each gauntlet followed the sinews of the arm and hand beneath. "Even through the boots, through the gloves, the muscle definition continues," he says, "and so you get this impression of a tower of strength." Incidentally, Wilkinson adds, "My favorite details of the Batsuit are the brass knuckles on the gloves."

MECH SUIT

With a godlike opponent comes the need for super-human protection. So, when Batman goes up against Superman one-on-one, he is forced to pull out the strongest armor in his arsenal – the Mech Suit. And, rather than resort to motion capture technology which would have allowed them to add in the cumbersome suit during post-production, the suit was actually built and used during filming. "We made a determination that we wanted to use the real Mech Suit," says producer Deborah Snyder. "Although, let me tell you, when you're in the rain, up on a rooftop shooting IMAX, it's not the most practical thing."

As with the regular Batsuit's cowl, the first stage of making the Mech Suit was a clay sculpt. "The suit is clearly inspired by Frank Miller's The Dark Knight Returns," says Zack Snyder, speaking of the acclaimed graphic novel, "but we were also having to drill down into the why of it. I believe that it was probably originally created for another reason – for riots that he had to deal with, maybe. So the suit was not specifically created to fight Superman, per se, but I think he's repurposed it. In this case he's really using it to buy time."

PRODUCTION

"We looked at the armor from that graphic novel, and what Zack liked about it is this sense that it's quite analog," says Michael Wilkinson. "You get the sense that it's something that a guy has put together – welded, prototyped – in his work room. It's unfinished and raw and oversized and a little brutish."

There were a few moments during filming when it became apparent that using the actual Mech Suit just wasn't practical. "Some of the fighting is extremely difficult," says Deborah Snyder, "so there are scenes where we did use the motion capture suit. But we tried whenever possible to go with the real thing. It definitely grounds the fight in reality. The way that Henry [Cavill] reacts to Ben [Affleck] when he's in that suit is different than if it was just a mo-cap suit."

"SUPERMAN HAS THESE AMAZING GODLIKE POWERS, AND BATMAN WOULD BE NO MATCH AGAINST HIM IF IT WERE NOT FOR THE TECHNOLOGY HE EXPLOITS."
DEBORAH SNYDER

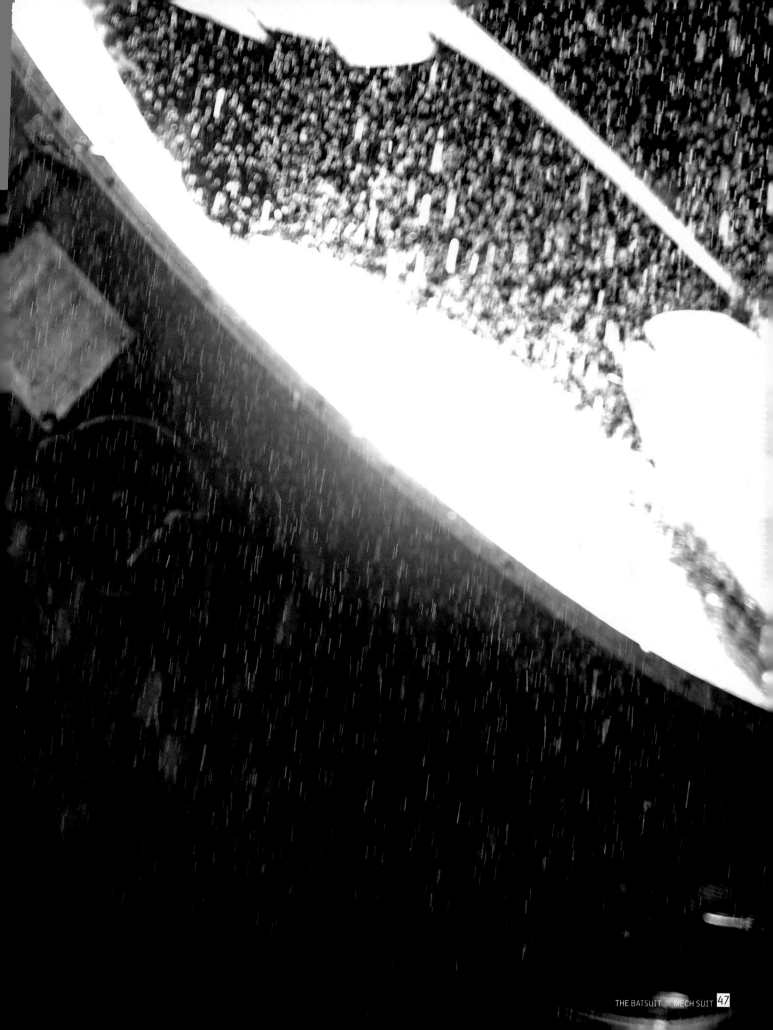

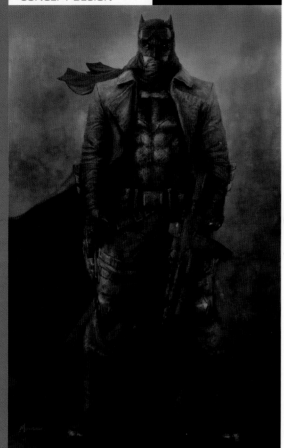

KNIGHTMARE BATMAN

Bruce Wayne's fears for what may happen if he can't find a way to neutralize Superman play out in an exploration of Batman's worst-case scenario. In a fevered dream-like sequence, a battered, dusty Batman makes his way through a devastated future, the harsh reality of this existence underlined by the changes to his costume. "The idea is that the suit evolved over time," says Zack Snyder, of the look he wanted Batman to adopt for this section of the film. "After some sort of apocalyptic disaster on Earth, that's what the cobbled-together Batsuit would be after a lot of practical, day-to-day living in it."

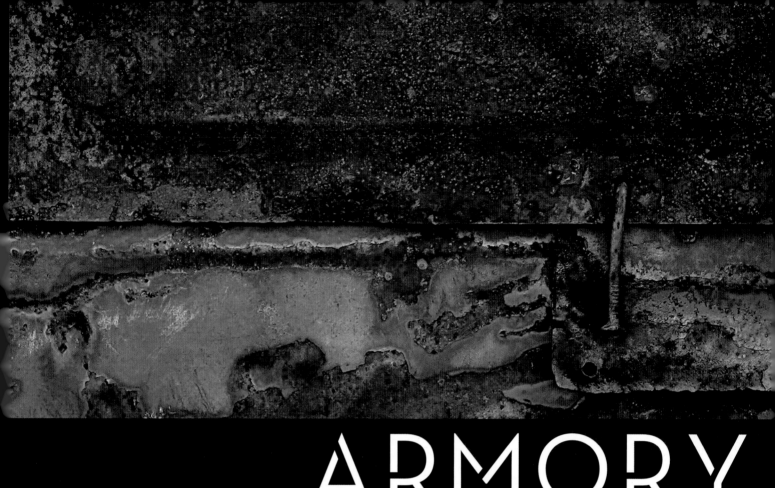

ARMORY

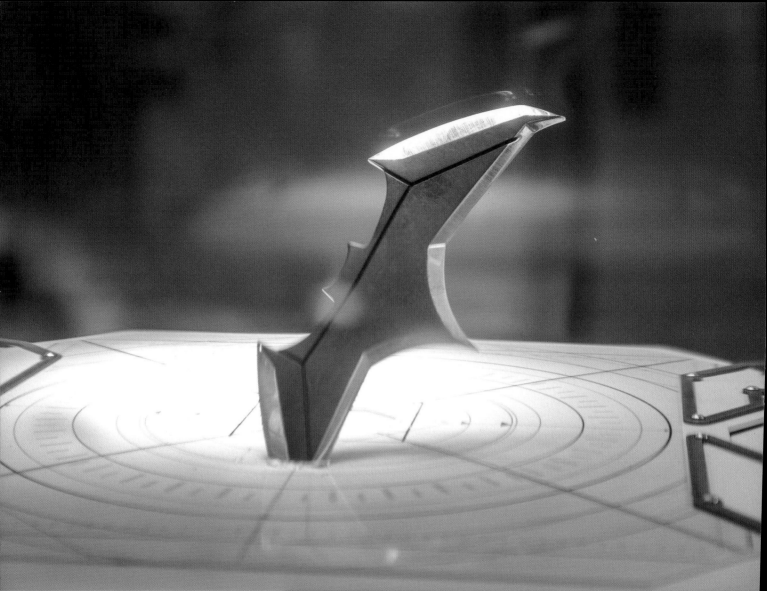

BATARANGS

"Batarangs are a staple for Batman, and they're in the signature bat form" says Zack Snyder. "He uses them to throw at assailants, he uses them as markers or calling cards. Some of them have incendiary tips, some of them can be used as a tracking device, and they have lethal striking ability." For Doug Harlocker, the Batarangs provided an opportunity to re-invent an iconic prop. "In past movies, the Batarangs were quite small," the prop master says. "They were these little things that he would pull out of his belt and throw. Zack gave us a lot of input, and we ended up retooling here and there. The scale grew to be probably twice the size of what we've seen in the past, and I think it really serves us."

CONCEPT DESIGN

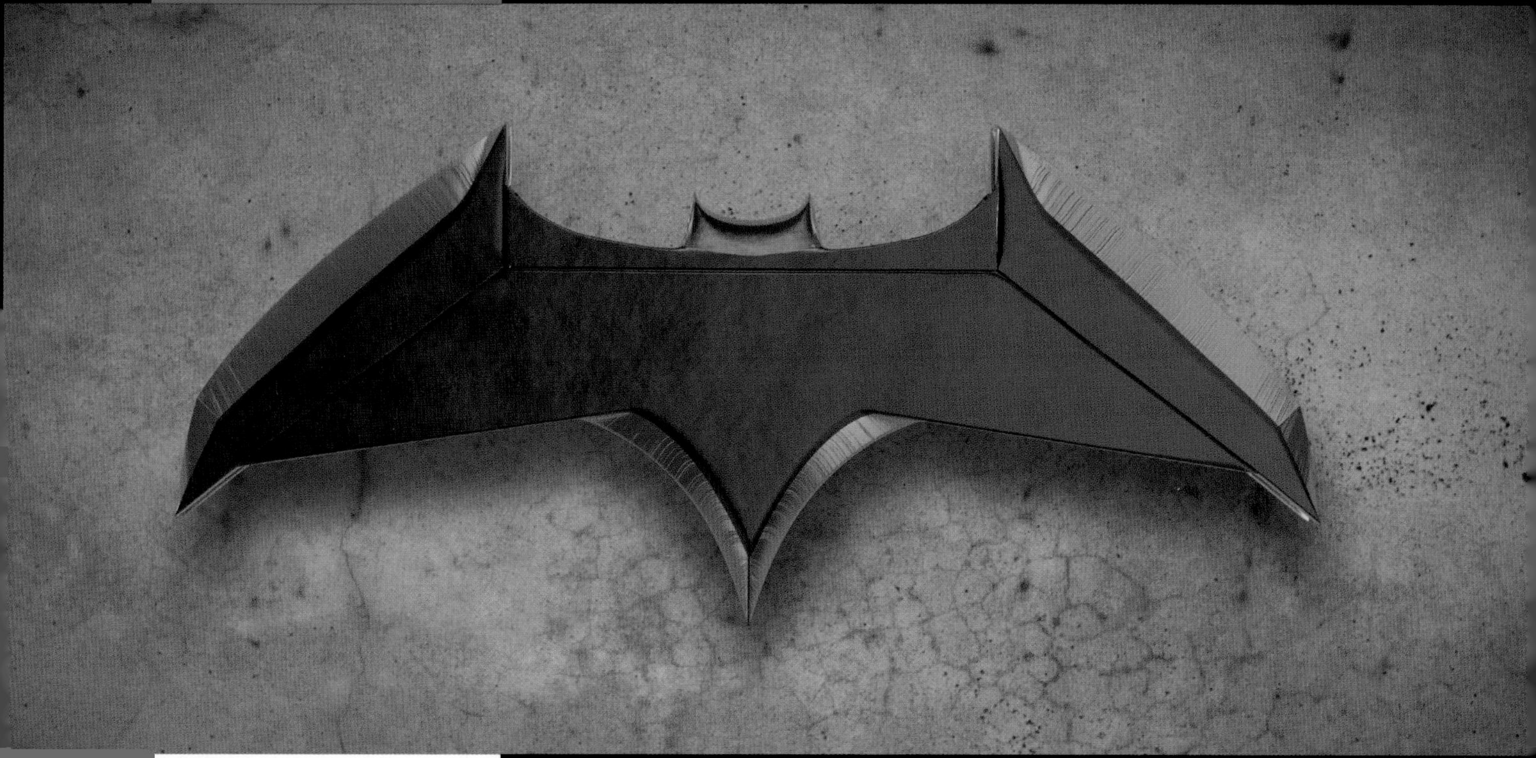

PRODUCTION

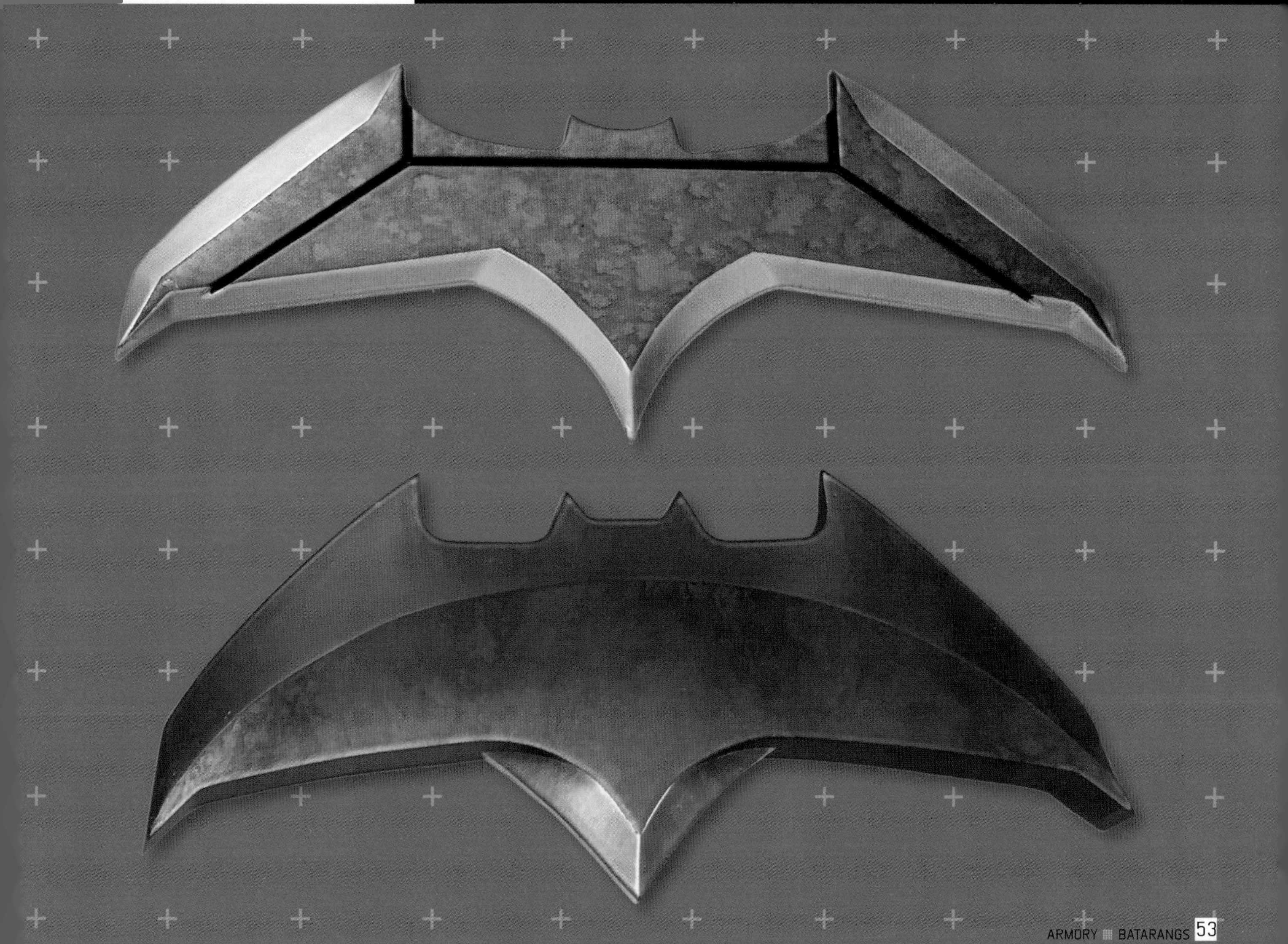

"WE MADE THEM OUT OF ALUMINUM. IT'S LIGHT AND EASY FOR THE ACTOR TO WORK WITH."

DOUG HARLOCKER

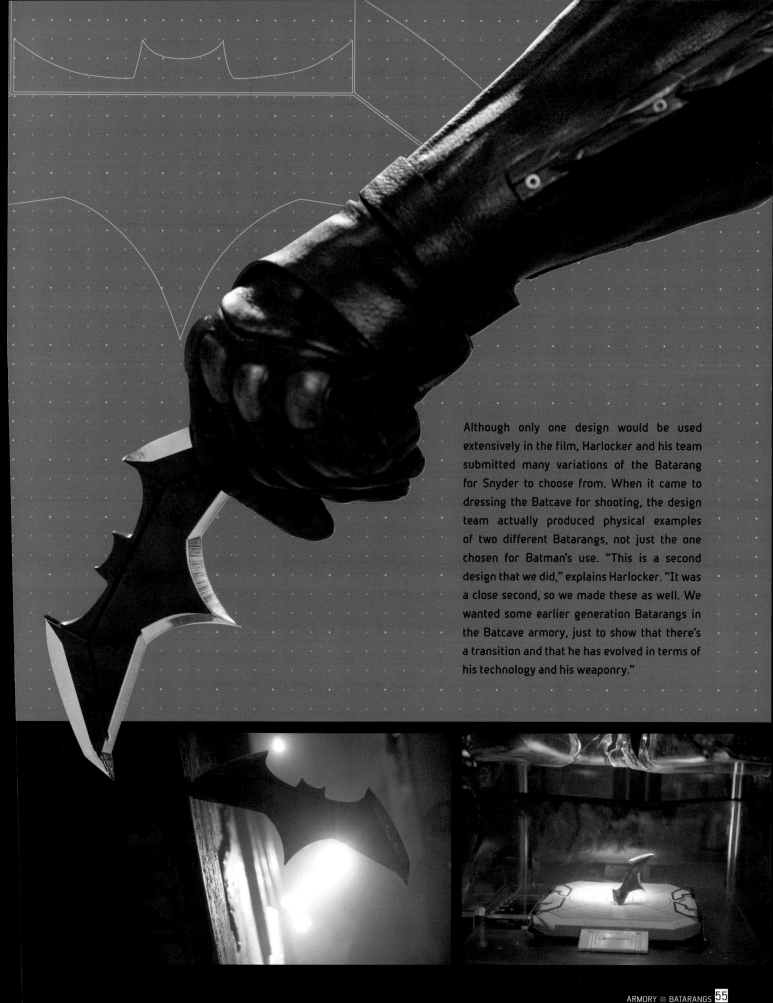

Although only one design would be used extensively in the film, Harlocker and his team submitted many variations of the Batarang for Snyder to choose from. When it came to dressing the Batcave for shooting, the design team actually produced physical examples of two different Batarangs, not just the one chosen for Batman's use. "This is a second design that we did," explains Harlocker. "It was a close second, so we made these as well. We wanted some earlier generation Batarangs in the Batcave armory, just to show that there's a transition and that he has evolved in terms of his technology and his weaponry."

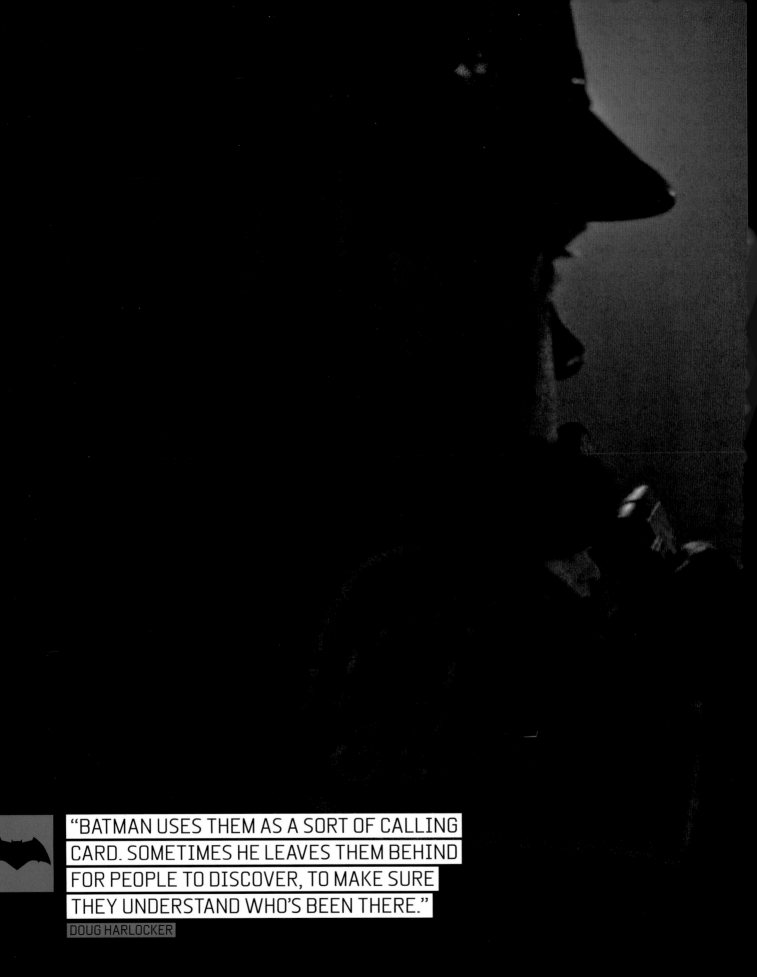

"BATMAN USES THEM AS A SORT OF CALLING CARD. SOMETIMES HE LEAVES THEM BEHIND FOR PEOPLE TO DISCOVER, TO MAKE SURE THEY UNDERSTAND WHO'S BEEN THERE."

DOUG HARLOCKER

BATBRAND

"Zack wanted to show the brutality and vigilantism of Batman," Doug Harlocker explains. "By permanently marking the worst of the worst, it's a warning to those out there of what they're dealing with. Zack thought the Batbrand should look a little bit like brass knuckles, but it had to have an electronic aspect that could heat up in a moment. It had to be small, something that could, in this case, fit in Bruce Wayne's pocket. We moulded the Bat symbol out of acrylic, then we painted that and put LEDs behind it, and put a dimmer on it so that when he presses a little micro switch, it comes up to a red hot glow. He can touch the switch again and it will come back to a cool feel. He could pull it out and it would heat up in a second, he could brand, pull it away and we could immediately see it die down to cold steel again."

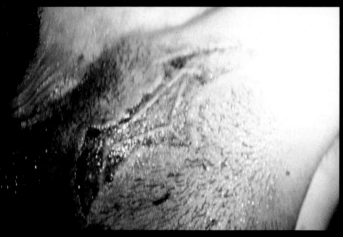

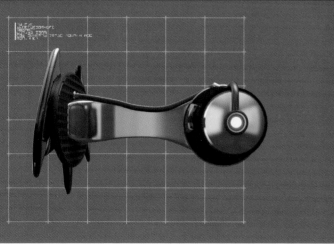

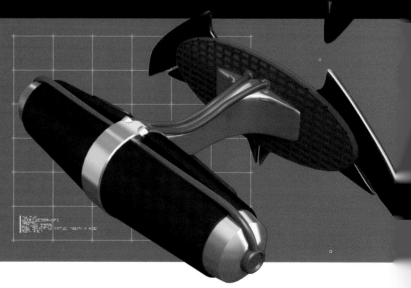

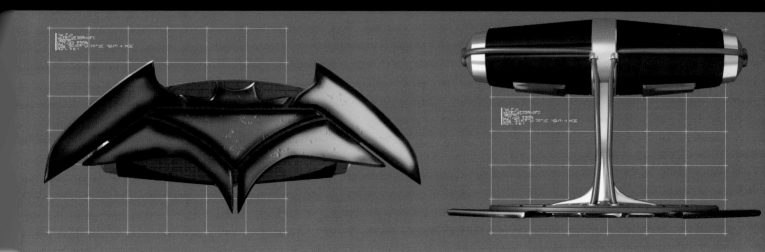

GRAPPLING GUN

"We designed half a dozen versions, and the two that Zack liked were miles apart in terms of design," explains Doug Harlocker, of how Batman ended up with two very different pieces of the same kit. "The gun-like version was originally all metallic with a carbon fiber handle. Zack focused on the handle a lot, because he wanted the bottom part to be more substantial, so that Batman could hit with it. He could use it as a weapon. So we added a return to the bottom of the grip that wrapped around his pinkie a little bit."

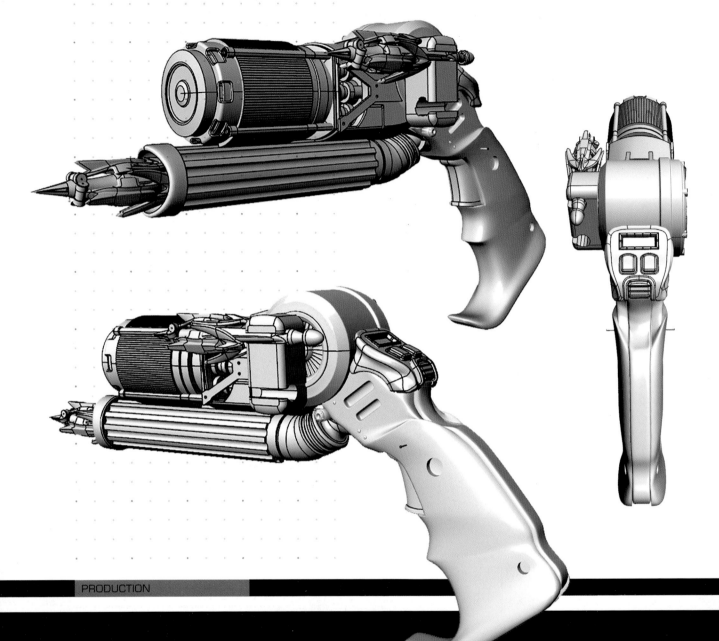

"We fabricated a bunch in aluminum with carbon fiber on the handle and everybody loved it, it was great," says Harlocker. "But then after about a week, Zack was looking at it and said, 'You know, I think the handle should be a wood grip that has some distress to it and some nicks in the wood. It's the difference between a synthetic weapon and something with wood furniture that you polish and take care of.' It's something I would never have thought of. So we switched them out and retooled the gun, and it was fabulous. It was like all of a sudden, it was exactly right. That was straight out of Zack. That wooden handle really made the prop."

"ZACK WANTED IT TO FEEL LIKE IT HAD BEEN AROUND FOR A COUPLE OF YEARS AND HE'D BEEN OUT IN THE FIELD WITH IT. IT'S A TRUSTED OLD FRIEND."

DOUG HARLOCKER

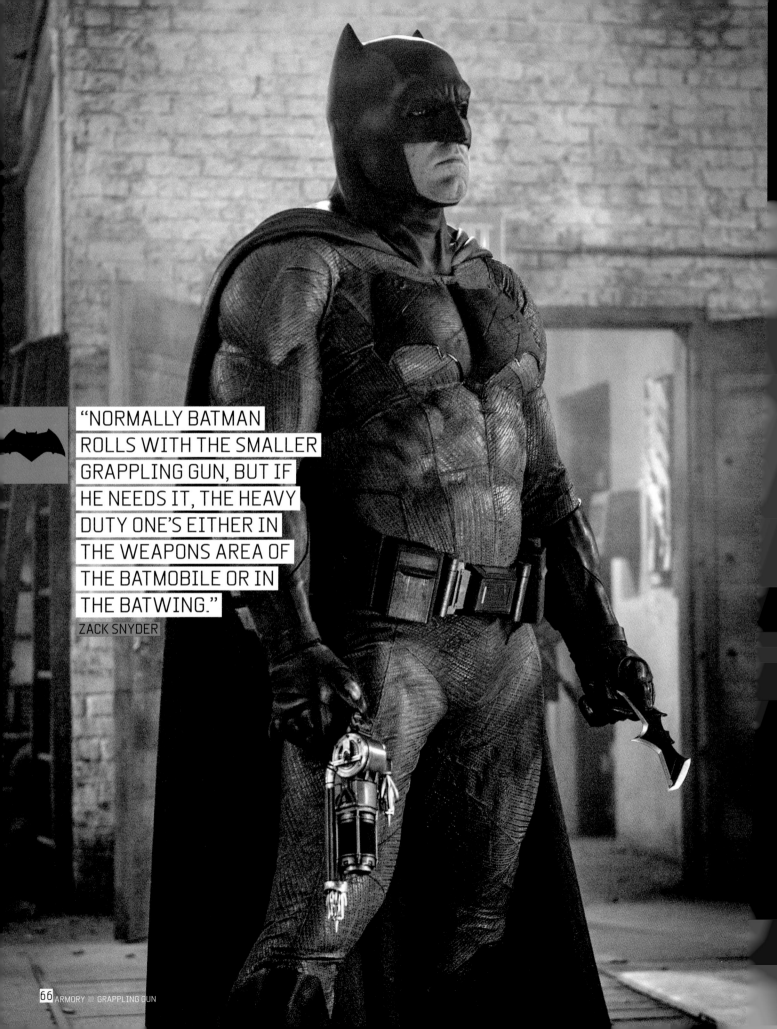

"NORMALLY BATMAN ROLLS WITH THE SMALLER GRAPPLING GUN, BUT IF HE NEEDS IT, THE HEAVY DUTY ONE'S EITHER IN THE WEAPONS AREA OF THE BATMOBILE OR IN THE BATWING."

ZACK SNYDER

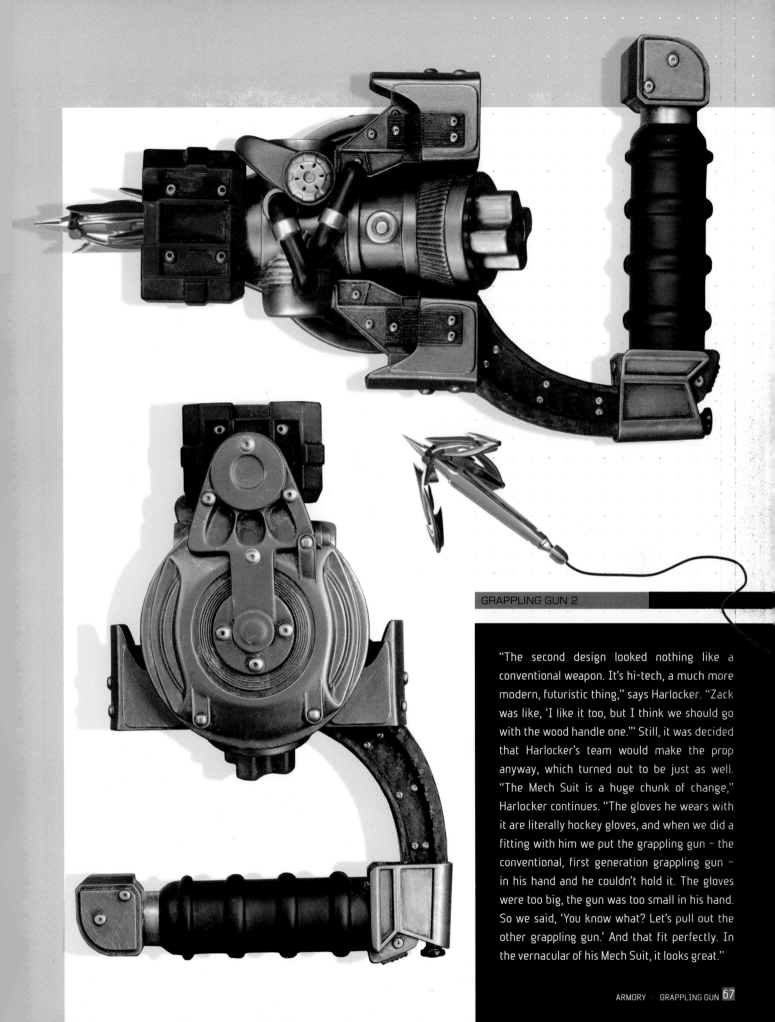

"The second design looked nothing like a conventional weapon. It's hi-tech, a much more modern, futuristic thing," says Harlocker. "Zack was like, 'I like it too, but I think we should go with the wood handle one.'" Still, it was decided that Harlocker's team would make the prop anyway, which turned out to be just as well. "The Mech Suit is a huge chunk of change," Harlocker continues. "The gloves he wears with it are literally hockey gloves, and when we did a fitting with him we put the grappling gun – the conventional, first generation grappling gun – in his hand and he couldn't hold it. The gloves were too big, the gun was too small in his hand. So we said, 'You know what? Let's pull out the other grappling gun.' And that fit perfectly. In the vernacular of his Mech Suit, it looks great."

"BATMAN USES HIS GRENADE LAUNCHER
TO FIRE GRENADES, SMOKE ROUNDS AND
KRYPTONITE ROUNDS."
ZACK SNYDER

H1204

GRENADE LAUNCHER

"We were doing research on grenade launchers and we found a picture of a very contemporary model," recalls Doug Harlocker. "I'd never seen it in a movie, and it really had a very Batman-ish feel to it. It was complicated, but not over-complicated, and the scale was really good for him – not too big, not too small. I presented it to Zack, who said, 'Yeah, that's great!' So we did some paint applications to it and modified the stock. It was a great looking thing."

GRENADES

Though the grenade launcher was adapted from real-world tech, Doug Harlocker and his team had to develop rounds to work with it that were specific to Batman's needs. "The grenades are Batman's attempt to weaponize certain things in order to foil Superman," says the props master. "He is basically using 40mm grenades as a foundation to weaponize these lethal things."

PRODUCTION

"The lead grenade was a hand grenade that we illustrated," says Harlocker. "That was meant to blow up and release a lot of lead. Superman can't see through lead walls, so it's to put a load of lead in the air to provide a distraction so that Batman could get close."

KRYPYONITE GRENADE

These grenades, tooled by Batman inside the Batcave, are designed to hold a quantity of the pulverised element fatal to Kryptonians. "He fires it at Superman, Superman is so fast that he catches the grenade in mid-air, but the grenade is supposed to immediately explode into a cloud of dust. It's not to penetrate, but by hitting him it would activate this mechanical catch and release this gas," explains Harlocker. "We made it with spring-loaded elements, so that when it springs open in his hand, and shows a series of gas ports and a light within, and then visual effects adds a gas element to it. We made those so that the actor could activate them in his hand or we had a cable release so that in case he couldn't move his finger in a close up, we could just pop it open for him."

STICKY BOMB

"It's a super-magnetic homing device," says Harlocker, of the sticky bomb. "The premise was that if Batman throws them, they'll find the closest metallic thing and blow it up. That's something we designed. It's a small magnetic piece – we had to make it a certain scale so that we could see it, and we added electronics to it, like a blinking red LED."

Sticky bombs sit beside a phone, showing the scale of these small but highly effective weapons.

"The concept is that it's something Batman could attach to any outgoing server cable and it would tap in and look for certain files to download," says Harlocker. "This was tricky, because it had to have a little functionality. We had to put a screen in it. Zack wanted it to be fairly small, and he wanted the screen to be able to play back. So we found the smallest LCD screen known to man at a frame rate that was good for camera with no pulsing and no tripping lines, and we backed that into a rugged metal design. We added multiple ports into it so that when Batman brought it back to the Batcave he could have a wiring harness from this little thing into his computer."

DIGITAL LEACH

LASER

Batman uses this laser to develop key weaponry and bolster his arsenal. "We wanted it to look like a traditional atom-buster, like the huge ones that are there in Europe, underground," Doug Harlocker explains. "They look a bit like a jet engine." As the prop developed, though, it exceeded anyone's expectations. "We started by making it fairly small, and it was supposed to be upstairs where Alfred works. But then we decided to put it downstairs in the Batcave, and realized it would look pretty diminutive in that space. So we scaled it up and it became a much bigger prop, something that Bruce could really interact with."

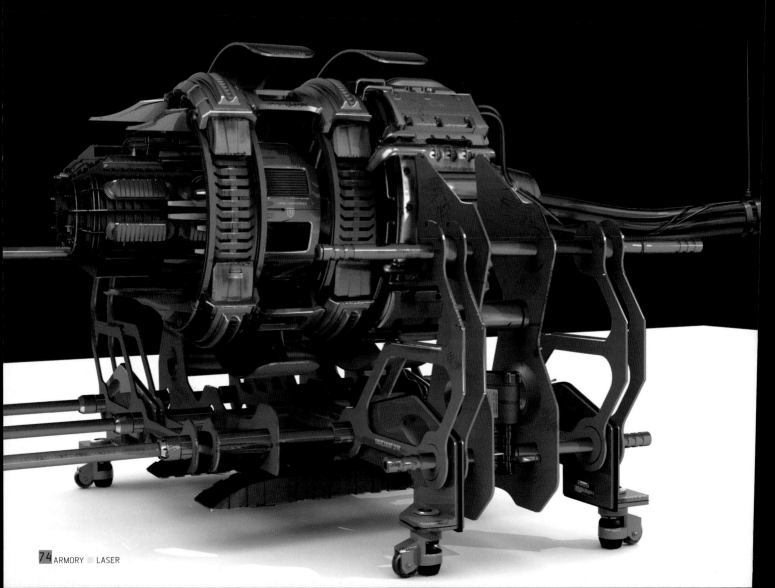

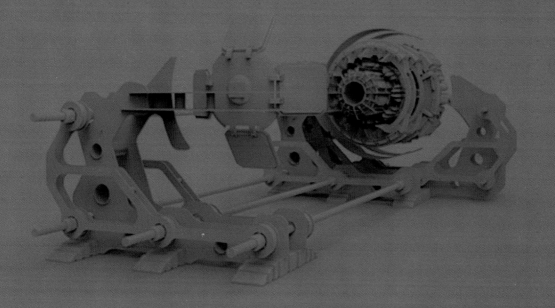

The scaled-up prop ended up being one of the biggest made for the entire shoot, weighing over 900 pounds. "Lewis Doty and I spit-balled it and 3D modeled it and then showed it to Zack," says Harlocker, of the development stage. "Zack made some modifications and we reverse-engineered and built it. We added aluminum, carbon fiber and metallics. We scorched it around where the laser was and added a whole lot of lights, and we put it on dimmers so that when he switched on the laser he could start it up in phases. We see the initial start up and then as the power increases he can keep hitting switches and things will grow and grow. I like making big props. This is impossible to miss – it's a beast!"

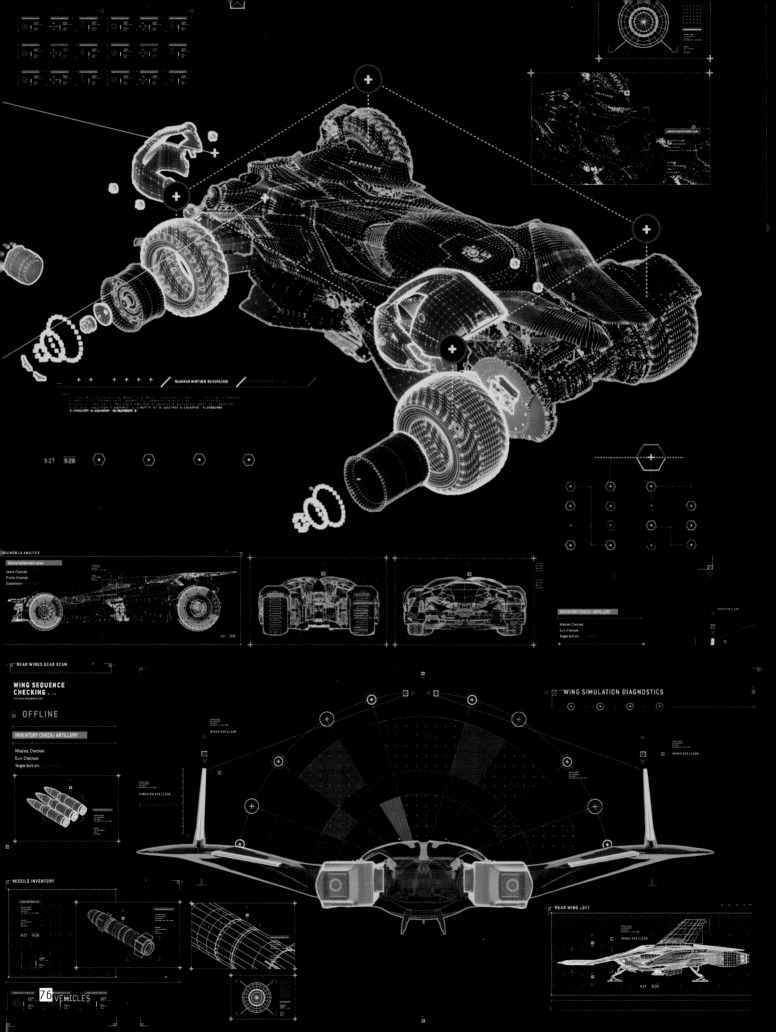

VEHICLES
...

BATWING

"I wanted it to have bat-like qualities, but not be too goofy," says Zack Snyder of his initial brief for Batman's airborne vehicle. "So we set about designing what I'd like to call a pretty cool and practical airplane. It has vertical take off and landing (VTOL) capabilities, it has foldable wings for storage, it's kind of modeled in some ways on a plane that might be able to go on an aircraft carrier. One of the mandates was that there would be no runway for it, so it had to be able to take off vertically."

CONCEPT DESIGN

"In the Batcave, I really wanted to have the Batwing hanging like a bat," explains production designer Patrick Tatopoulos. "The idea of creating a big tarp was to not reveal it too soon – this helped us to hide most of the body of the Batwing." After experimenting with various fabrics, the tarp itself was eventually made from latex. "It feels almost like a membrane, it's very organic, it's super-heavy. But it fits everything and wrinkles in a phenomenal way."

Patrick Tatopoulos was in complete agreement with the director about how the Batwing should launch. "A vertical take off is a must for Batman," he says. "To me it's part of the technology Batman should have. I wanted the wings to flip, so he can land anywhere and narrow the wingspan to go anywhere he wants – into an alley, for example. And then there is the movement – it changes shape in the sky and that is very cool."

CONCEPT DESIGN

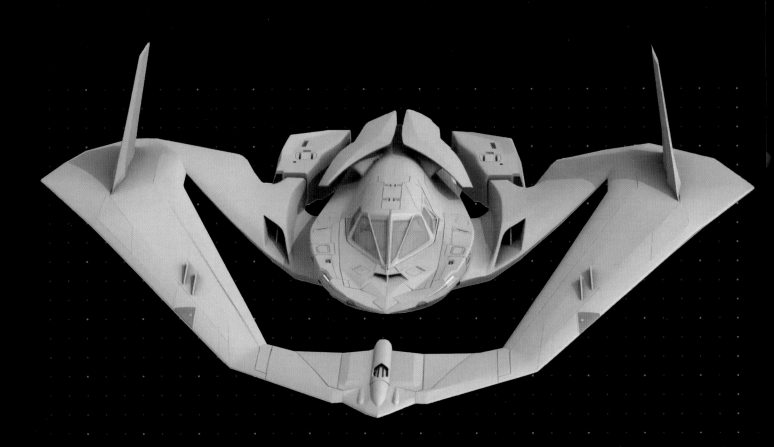

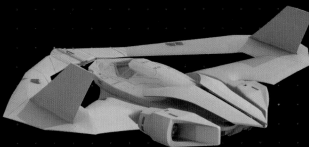

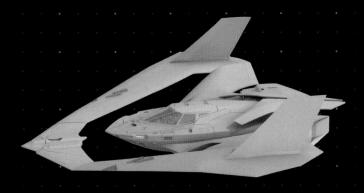

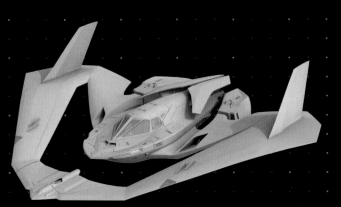

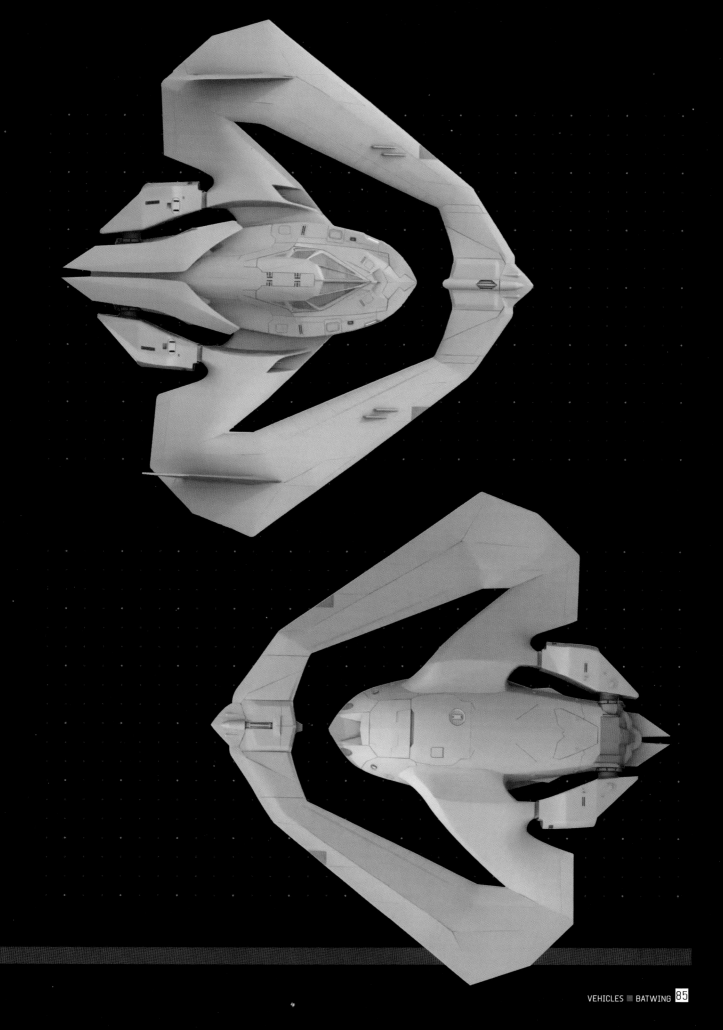

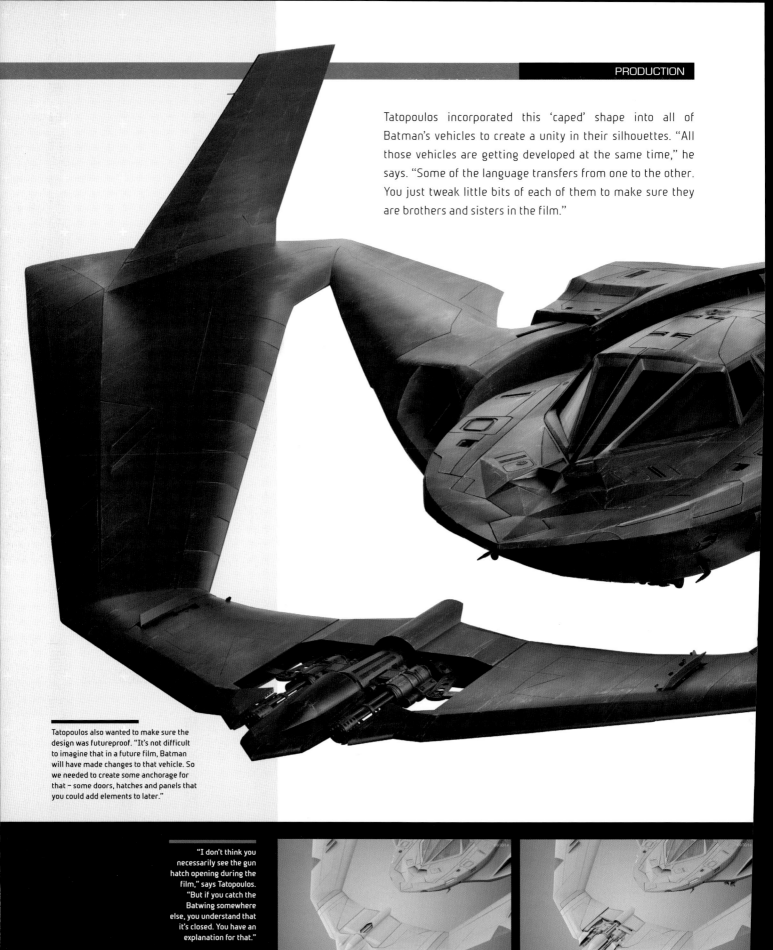

Tatopoulos incorporated this 'caped' shape into all of Batman's vehicles to create a unity in their silhouettes. "All those vehicles are getting developed at the same time," he says. "Some of the language transfers from one to the other. You just tweak little bits of each of them to make sure they are brothers and sisters in the film."

Tatopoulos also wanted to make sure the design was futureproof. "It's not difficult to imagine that in a future film, Batman will have made changes to that vehicle. So we needed to create some anchorage for that – some doors, hatches and panels that you could add elements to later."

"I don't think you necessarily see the gun hatch opening during the film," says Tatopoulos. "But if you catch the Batwing somewhere else, you understand that it's closed. You have an explanation for that."

"That's one big rotary machine gun," says Tatopoulos of the Batwing's main weapon. "It's a bit like the classic airplane from WW1, with the propeller in the front – the idea is that the machine gun rotates. Because what I wanted was to hide the gun completely so that it's folded into its own shell, and then it lifts up and the rotary machine gun starts shooting."

"IT HAS A MACHINE GUN, IT HAS MISSILES, IT'S FAST: IT SHOULD BE ABLE TO GET BATMAN FROM POINT A TO POINT B RATHER QUICKLY."
ZACK SNYDER

"What's important for you as a designer is if someone says, 'How did that happen?' you're able to answer those questions," Tatopoulos adds. "You need to create an object that has got its own reason to be built that way."

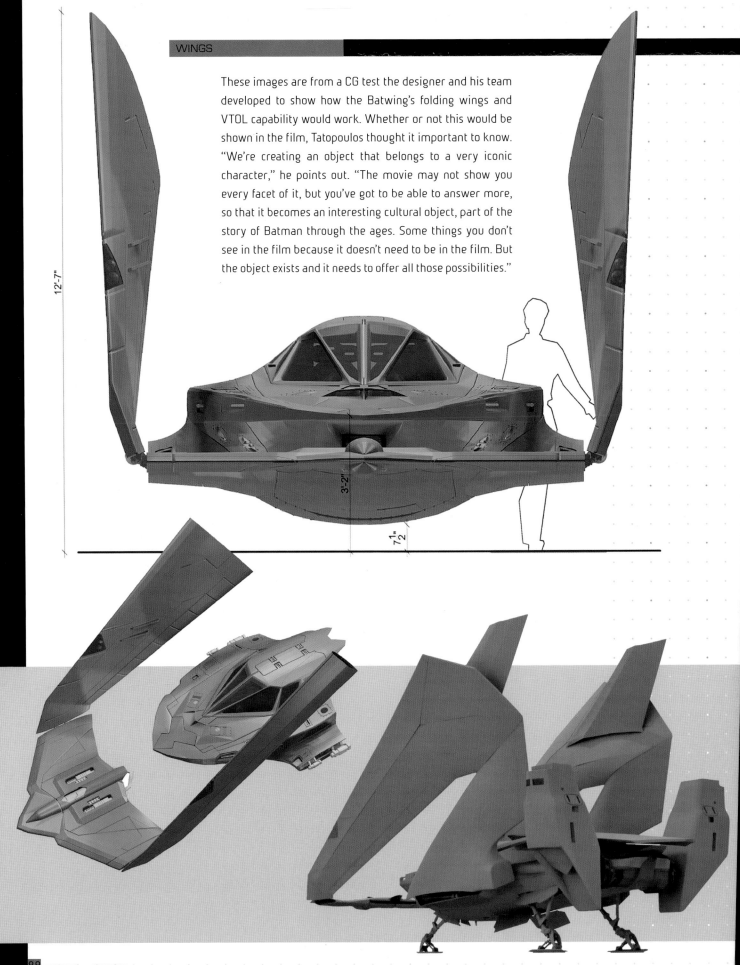

These images are from a CG test the designer and his team developed to show how the Batwing's folding wings and VTOL capability would work. Whether or not this would be shown in the film, Tatopoulos thought it important to know. "We're creating an object that belongs to a very iconic character," he points out. "The movie may not show you every facet of it, but you've got to be able to answer more, so that it becomes an interesting cultural object, part of the story of Batman through the ages. Some things you don't see in the film because it doesn't need to be in the film. But the object exists and it needs to offer all those possibilities."

12'-7"

3'-2"

7'-2"

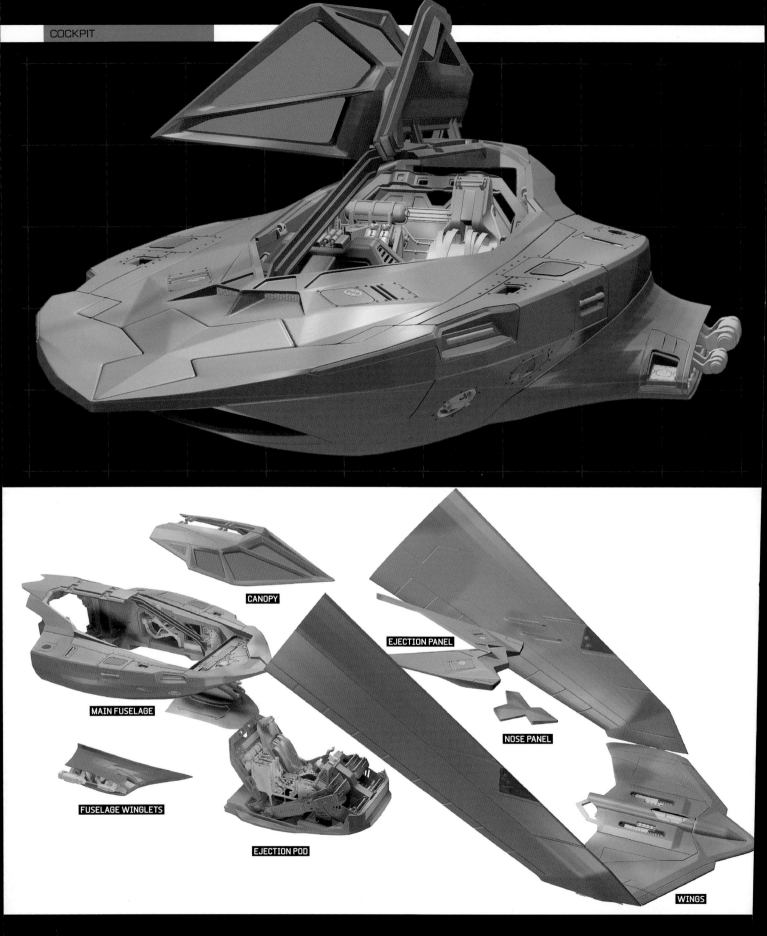

CANOPY

EJECTION PANEL

MAIN FUSELAGE

NOSE PANEL

FUSELAGE WINGLETS

EJECTION POD

WINGS

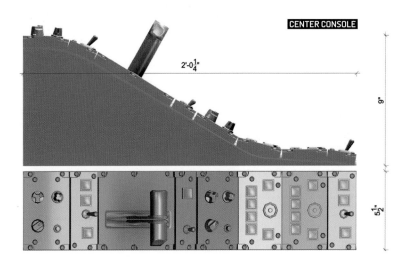

2'-0$\frac{1}{4}$"

9"

5$\frac{1}{2}$"

"We used instrumentation from jet fighters and created our own as well," says Tatopoulos, of the cockpit. "And we started with a two-seater, but quickly we realised that because of the situation that is in this film, we can seat two people, but the second seat is basically an armory."

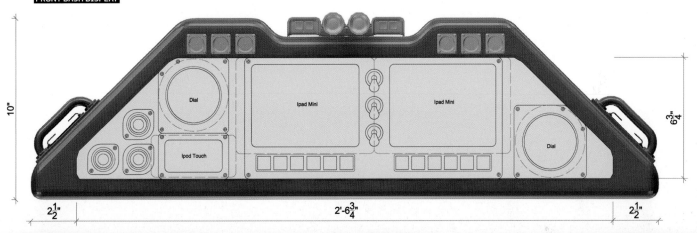

FRONT DASH DISPLAY

10"

6$\frac{3}{4}$"

Dial

Ipad Mini

Ipad Mini

Ipod Touch

Dial

2$\frac{1}{2}$"

2'-6$\frac{3}{4}$"

2$\frac{1}{2}$"

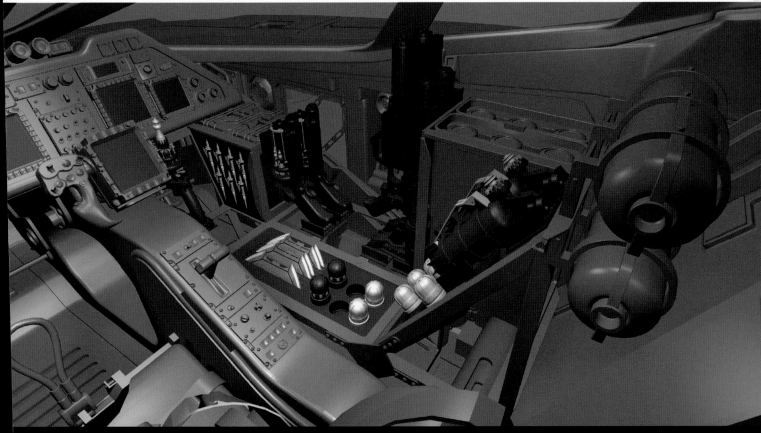

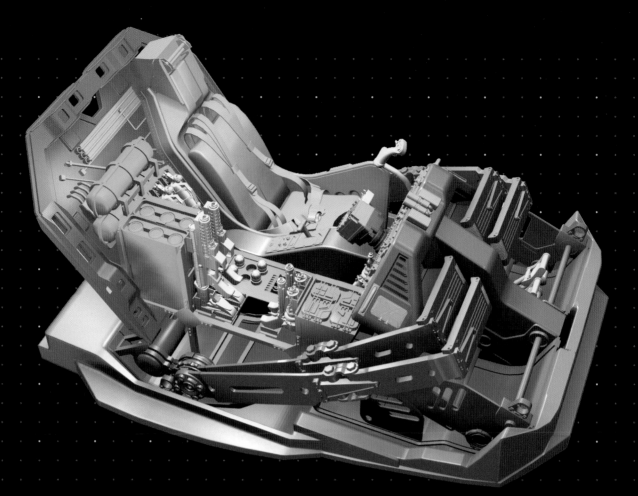
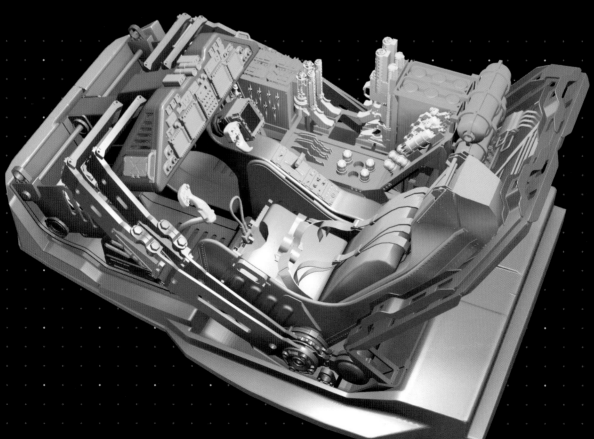

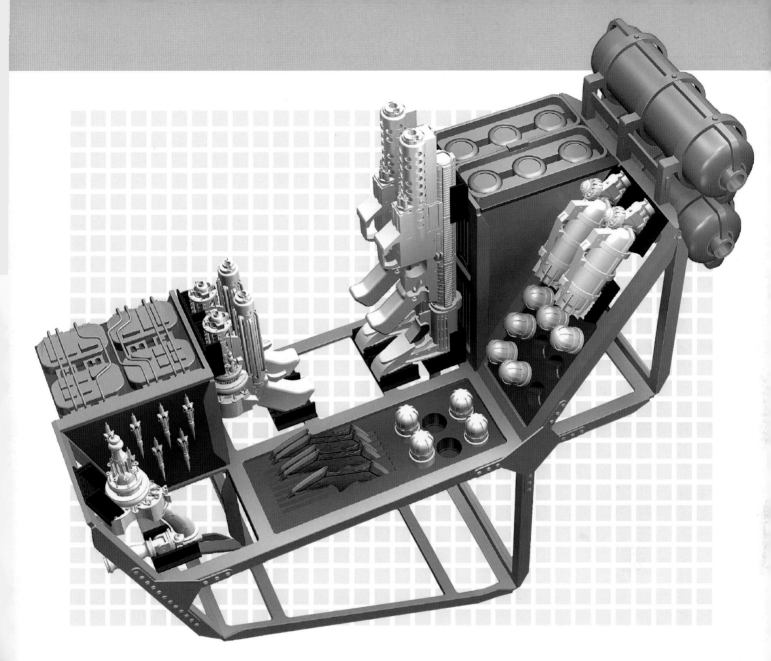

WEAPON RACK

The modification of the second seat feeds into the idea of a Bruce Wayne who maintains his own vehicles purely as utilities for his crime fighting. He's taken that disused space and made it useful rather than redesigning it to create a more aesthetic vehicle. For Zack Snyder, this decision also has another significance that adds to his vision of this Batman's character. "Of course, Robin was around in earlier incarnations. Bruce took out the seat and put more guns in there. I think that's a psychological reaction to losing a family member, a confidant."

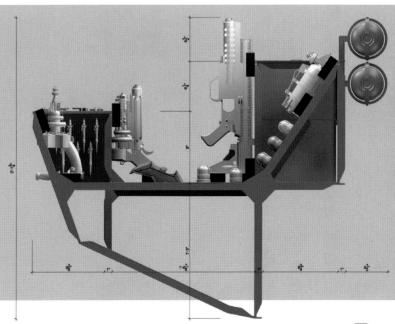

Aside from the parts Tatopoulos's team built to be seen when the Batwing was at rest in the Batcave, the wings of the aircraft were entirely computer rendered. "For the Batmobile we of course built a whole practical driving machine, but with the Batwing that wasn't necessary, because there would be so much VFX," explains Snyder. "But we did build a cockpit and canopy that we could shoot from the outside."

"There's a moment where the Batwing crashes," adds Tatopoulos. "I talked to Zack and suggested that maybe the body of the Batwing snaps – the cockpit pulls as he crashes and separates itself from the rest of the Batwing. So now the CG part of the Batwing is out of our shot – we don't have to worry about it, and the crashed part is only the cockpit. So we did a destroyed version of it that sits against the building and that was also a practical set. I was very, very pleased with this one. Between the carpenters, the sculptors and the painting, it came together well."

BATMOBILE

Production designer Patrick Tatopoulos is a self-confessed petrol head. He loves powerful cars and Superbikes. So it's not surprising that his starting point for the aesthetic of the entire film was the Batmobile itself. "You always need to start with something," he says. "The car was the obvious choice." Tatopoulos came straight out of his first meeting with Zack Snyder, sat down in a coffee shop and sketched out his initial ideas for Batman's new wheels. "He told me very early on is that this is going to be a bolder, slightly older guy," says the designer. "Just these few words from Zack were enough. I went into something that's more like an off-road car. I wanted the whole top of the car to be one very hard line, almost like a cape that's sitting on top of an engine and wheels. That's why the top profile of the car is very settled. It's almost like a wedge. The way the front of the vehicle is lower than the back, that whole aggressive look."

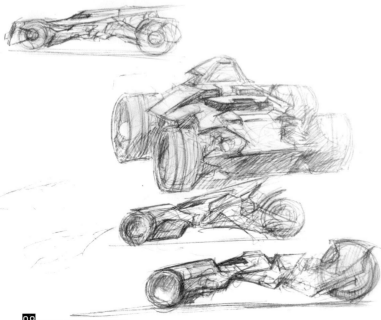

Once he and concept artist Ed Natividad had created a design the director was happy with, Tatopoulos employed Dennis McCarthy and his team to actually build the car, with Kevin Ishioka coming on board as art director. "What appealed to me about Dennis is not the fact that he can build cars, but the fact that he raced off-road cars as well," says Tatopoulos. McCarthy knew exactly what he needed to do to realize Tatopoulos's concept. "I brought in the best fabricators that I know, guys that have the same background that I do," says McCarthy. "If you can build an off-road car that can withstand the Baja 1000 or a shore course race, you can build a picture car that's going to live. That's really one of the key elements of the Batmobile, its durability factor. Everything on it is overbuilt."

Tatopoulos's earliest pencil sketches for the Batmobile (below) show just how close the finished vehicle remained to his original ideas. The designer lists motorcycles, Formula 1 cars and jet fighters as his inspiration for the car's shape. Concept artist Ed Natividad worked closely with Tatopoulos to refine the design.

CONCEPT DESIGN

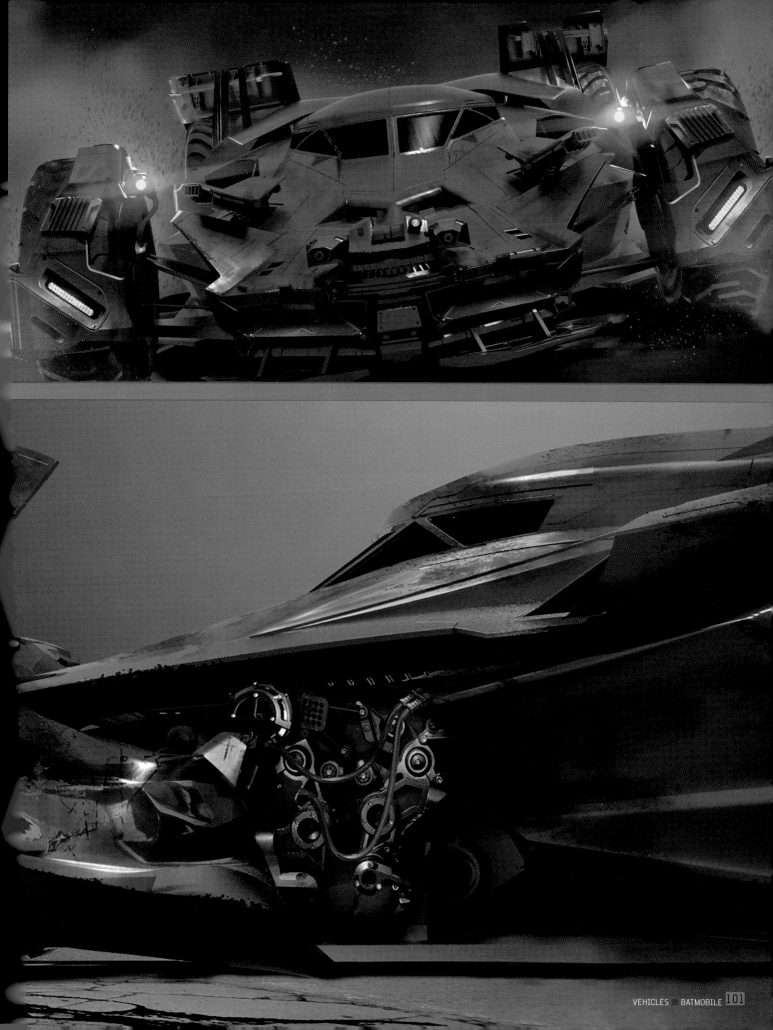

CONCEPT DESIGN

The Batmobile's variable suspension was a must for Tatopoulos. "The suspension was really my first concept," he says. "I've seen Batmobiles through the generations, jumping in the street and landing hard, and they're fabulous looking, but you can tell those cars were not meant to jump. I decided early on that I wanted this car to be able to have a raised and lowered suspension, so we could have a car that, when it jumps, it lands in a very elegant way."

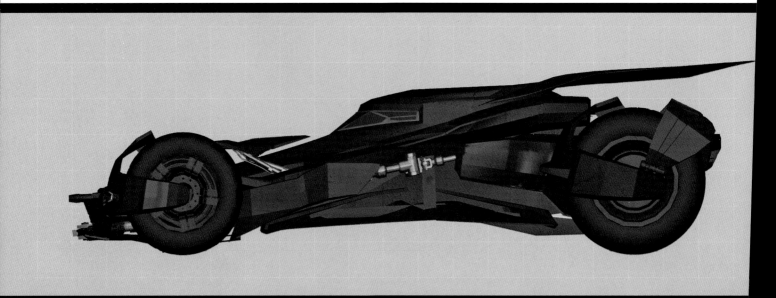

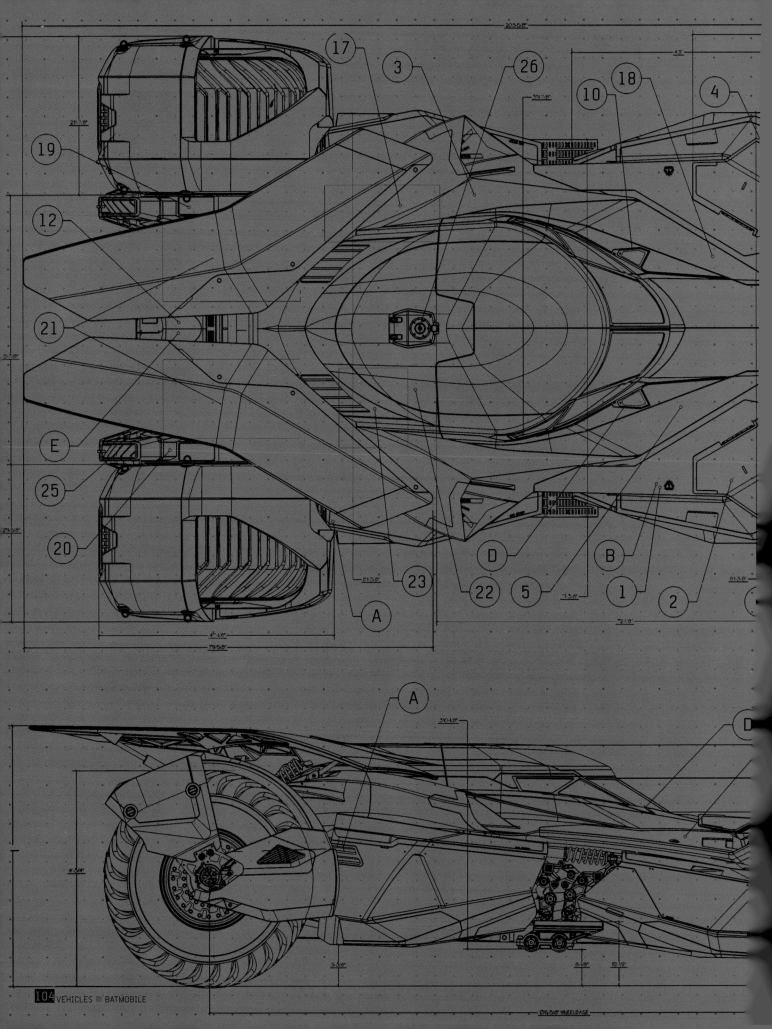

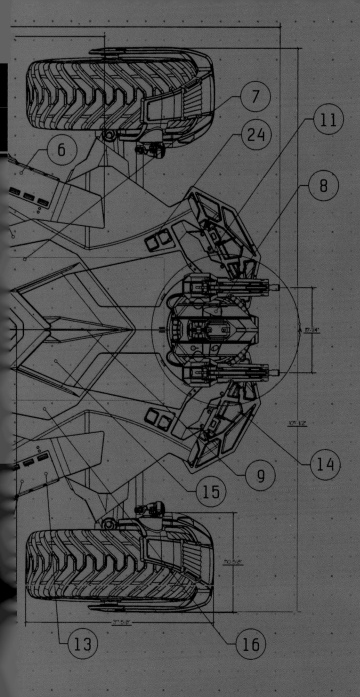

1	Electrified Skin Deterrent
2	Concealment Smoke Grenade Launcher System
3	Anti-roll System
4	Shield Generator Housing
5	Jamming Signal System
6	Ballistic Missile Defense System
7	Electromagnetic Pulse Protection

MODIFICATION	
A	Vaporized Effluvium Kryptonite
B	Infused Kryptonite Skin Coating

ARMAMENT SYSTEMS	
8	Heat Ray Crowd Control Dispersal Cannon
9	Main Weapons Bay
10	Sound Compliance Non-Lethal System
11	Xenon Stun/Spot Searchlights
12	Secondary Weapons Bay
13	Anti-Material Missile Weapon
14	Cow Catcher

MODIFICATION	
C	Direct Kryptonite Vapor Trajectile System
D	Kryptonite Transit Wave Emitter
E	Class 4 Cell Kryp.

MISCELLANEOUS COMPONENT AND SYSTEMS	
15	Thrust Vent (Forward)
16	Electronic Stabilizaion
17	Nitro-Methane Tank
18	Immobiliser
19	Muffler Bearings
20	Turbothrust Kinetic Ion Pulse Drives
21	Turbine
22	Dogleg
23	Secondary Nitro-Methane Tank
24	Helicopter Lifting Hooks
25	Exhaust Ports
26	Air-to-Ground Refuelling (AGR)

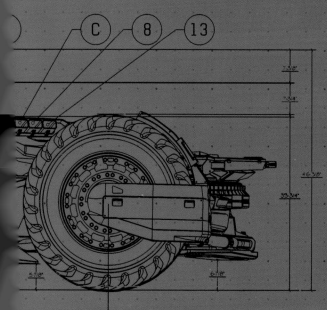

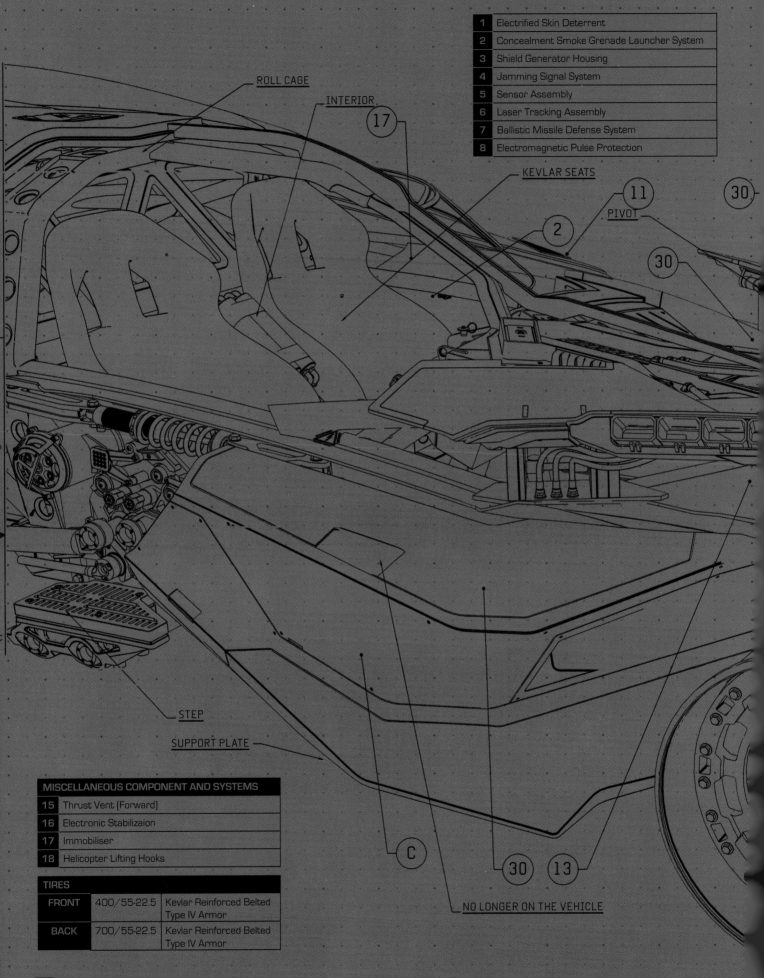

ROLL CAGE

INTERIOR

17

1	Electrified Skin Deterrent
2	Concealment Smoke Grenade Launcher System
3	Shield Generator Housing
4	Jamming Signal System
5	Sensor Assembly
6	Laser Tracking Assembly
7	Ballistic Missile Defense System
8	Electromagnetic Pulse Protection

KEVLAR SEATS

11

PIVOT

30

2

30

30

STEP

SUPPORT PLATE

C

30   13

NO LONGER ON THE VEHICLE

MISCELLANEOUS COMPONENT AND SYSTEMS	
15	Thrust Vent (Forward)
16	Electronic Stabilizaion
17	Immobiliser
18	Helicopter Lifting Hooks

TIRES		
FRONT	400/55-22.5	Kevlar Reinforced Belted Type IV Armor
BACK	700/55-22.5	Kevlar Reinforced Belted Type IV Armor

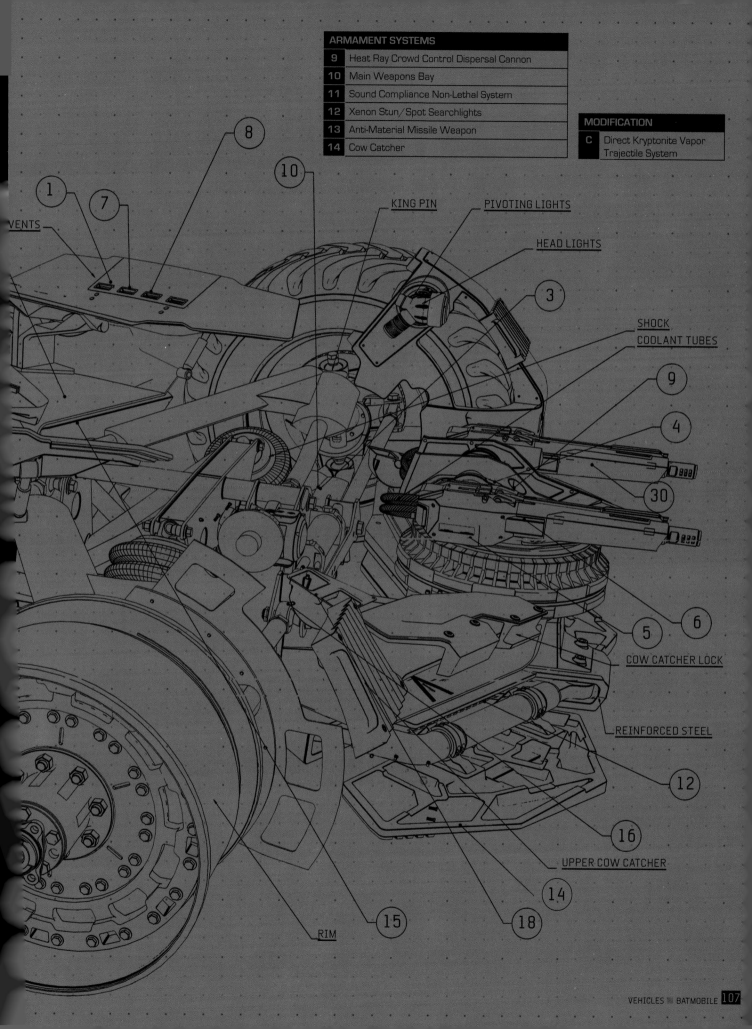

ARMAMENT SYSTEMS	
9	Heat Ray Crowd Control Dispersal Cannon
10	Main Weapons Bay
11	Sound Compliance Non-Lethal System
12	Xenon Stun / Spot Searchlights
13	Anti-Material Missile Weapon
14	Cow Catcher

MODIFICATION	
C	Direct Kryptonite Vapor Trajectile System

KING PIN

PIVOTING LIGHTS

HEAD LIGHTS

VENTS

SHOCK
COOLANT TUBES

COW CATCHER LOCK

REINFORCED STEEL

UPPER COW CATCHER

RIM

PRODUCTION

"We didn't have the time to build a mock-up of the car," says Tatopoulos. "This is where it was important to work with a team of people, because we could move forward together and play with the shape, with the detail, with every technical assembly part of the car as it was getting built. We did all the very early stages of the car-building in Los Angeles, and I was there at the shop every two days."

The Batmobile under construction. Tatopoulos and McCarthy chose the most powerful engine ever sold for road use in the United States. The huge rear tires are taken from a tractor with the treads shaved down.

"YOU'RE TALKING ABOUT AN AGGRESSIVE VEHICLE THAT'S GOING TO GO OUT AND WRANGLE SOME JUSTICE. I REMEMBER PATRICK AND I SAYING, 'YEAH – THIS FEELS LIKE IT COULD LEAVE A MARK.'"

ZACK SNYDER

"THIS BATMOBILE WAS PURPOSE-BUILT. IT'S THE CAR HE NEEDED FOR THE WORK OF BEING BATMAN. THAT ALLOWS IT TO BE A LITTLE MORE BAT-CENTRIC THAN IF IT WAS A FOUND OBJECT."

ZACK SNYDER

NO STEP

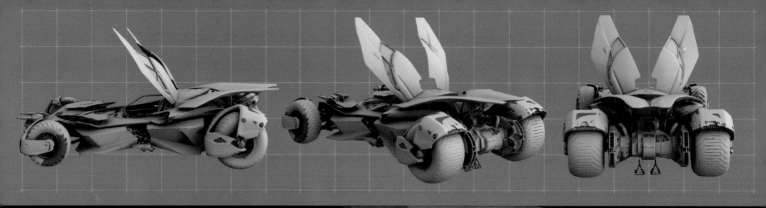

> ## "THIS THING IS SO BAD-ASS, AND IT ALSO RUNS LIKE YOU WOULD NOT BELIEVE. IT SOUNDS INCREDIBLE."
> DEBORAH SNYDER

Another unique design element of the Batmobile is in its doors, a specific idea Tatopoulos wanted to incorporate from the beginning. "The Batcave is all suspended, the way a bat is," he points out. "It was important to carry on that subliminal idea of a bat everywhere. I thought it would be great to have the doors open that way because it creates the wings of the bat when it's open. That allowed me to create a vision – you see it with the wings up in the Batcave and it just creates an extra shape. It becomes something else in the dark."

For Tatopoulos, seeing his designs come together was a high point: "When the Batmobile arrived in the Batcave and drove onto the catwalk all the way to the garage – that was the best moment for me."

COCKPIT

The analogy to a Formula 1 car is also seen in the Batmobile's steering wheel, just one of the numerous technical aspects of the car's cockpit interior. "We didn't want it to be refined, a clean, neat dashboard,"

"We wanted to make sure it had guns," says Snyder, of the capabilities he thought it important for the Batmobile to possess. "And that if you touched it, you could be electrified. We wanted to make sure that it had some sort of rockets that could launch if need be – you don't see those in the movie, but they're under panels. We wanted to make sure that it has a grappling hook, which we feel is very Batman-ish. It also has countermeasures in case you're fired at by, say, a rocket launcher or a missile."

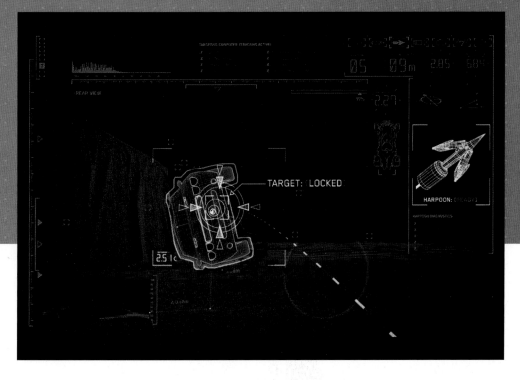

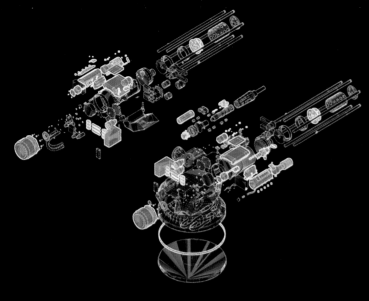

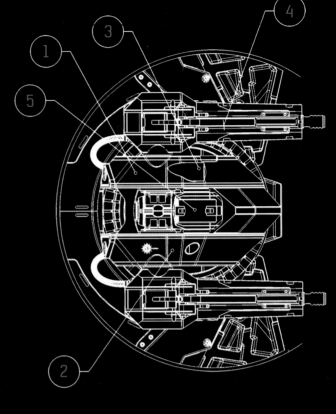

One of the most prominent aspects of the Batmobile is the machine gun assembly fitted to its nose. In the style of this bolder, harder Batman, the weapon is there for the world to see. "One thing that I was talking to Zack about was, 'Do you want the machine gun to retract itself into the car or just stay outside?'" recalls Tatopoulos. "Zack was very keen on keeping the machine gun outside all the time. That became a big part of its personality, because it's a very strong, balanced machine gun in the front. This was based on real modern weaponry as well, so it's not just a fantasy weapon. When we put it on the car I realized this is a great feature. Because Batman takes this car to go on a mission – he doesn't take it to go date a girl! This is something he's going to use for a purpose."

GUN TURRET - TOP VIEW	
1	Sensor Assembly
2	Laser Tracking Assembly
3	Heat Ray Crowd Control Dispersal Cannon
4	12.7x108mm Anti-material Weapon
5	Gyro Stabilization Assembly

GUN TURRET

"That turret can be removed and that's another element of the car," the designer explains. "There are a lot of panels and recesses in that car, because I know that in future there will be a need for more. So it is already set up to have modular elements adapted, or actually set into the body of the car, ready to come out – like anti-missile or lasers and so forth. It's all in the car already."

ON SCREEN

After two tests, one in the Californian desert and one in the snows of Detroit, Tatopoulos and McCarthy declared the Batmobile ready for the set. The production actually built two Batmobiles for filming, one with a full interior cockpit and one with just the basics for when it was required for stunt driving – which, of course, was often. Though CGI would be sparingly employed for some of the more violent maneuvers, the car's capabilities and handling had been engineered and set up so well that Zack Snyder could get exactly the shots he wanted while stunt driver Mike Justus was at the wheel.

"YOU NEVER EXPECT YOUR FANTASY VEHICLE TO ACTUALLY BE ABLE TO PERFORM IN SHOOTING SCENARIOS, BUT WE WERE AMAZED BY ITS AGILITY AND SPEED."

ZACK SNYDER

Justus was not only completely confident in the car and its abilities, but also completely bowled over by the vehicle's finish, calling it "sheer artistry." "It's a one-off car, high performance, set up to handle, set up to slide, functional, tough and powerful," he says. "It's an amazing car, and super fun to drive!"

BATCAVE
...

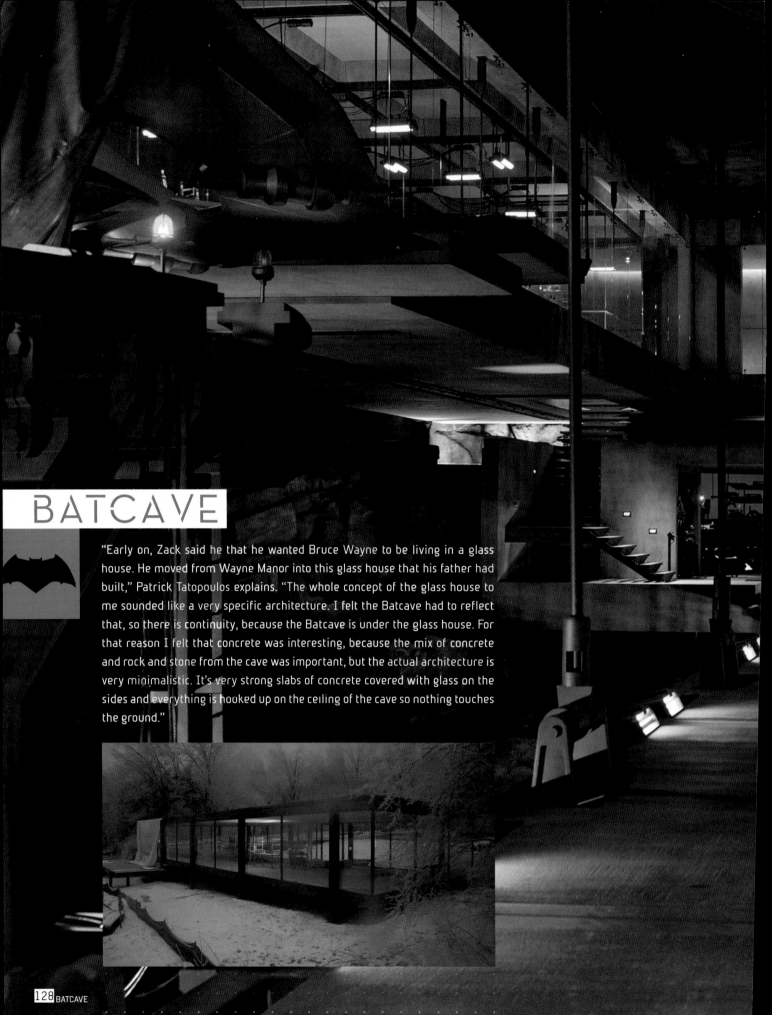

BATCAVE

"Early on, Zack said he that he wanted Bruce Wayne to be living in a glass house. He moved from Wayne Manor into this glass house that his father had built," Patrick Tatopoulos explains. "The whole concept of the glass house to me sounded like a very specific architecture. I felt the Batcave had to reflect that, so there is continuity, because the Batcave is under the glass house. For that reason I felt that concrete was interesting, because the mix of concrete and rock and stone from the cave was important, but the actual architecture is very minimalistic. It's very strong slabs of concrete covered with glass on the sides and everything is hooked up on the ceiling of the cave so nothing touches the ground."

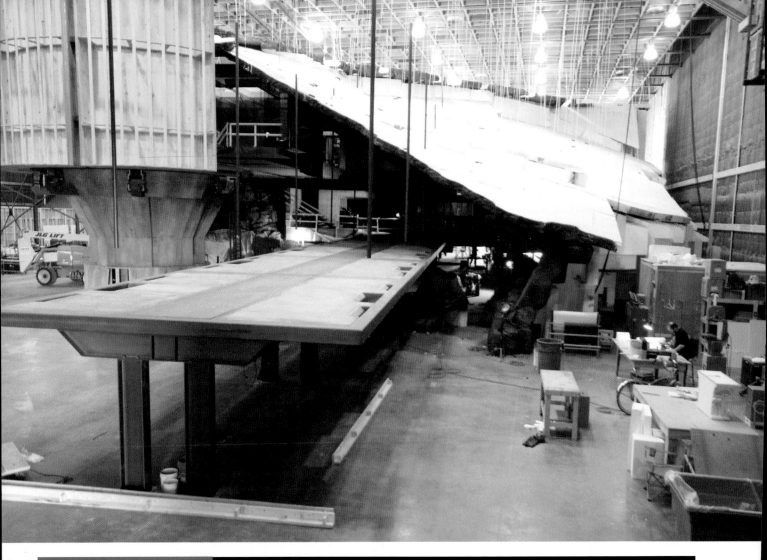

When it came to taking Tatopoulos's vision from the page to the stage, the production designer decided to build this hanging structure – for real. "We didn't have any green supports underneath," he says. "We built everything cantilevered so we had a real set completely finished, a gigantic structure that an entire crew would walk in, totally suspended, just all hanging in there. It was pretty crazy. This whole idea was to offer the director [the opportunity] of shooting from any angle of the set. The Batcave was built so that almost from every point of view you could see Batman travelling through the entire cave without changing your camera position."

ARMORY

WALK WAY

GARAGE

ACCESS TUNNEL

BATWING

LABORATORY

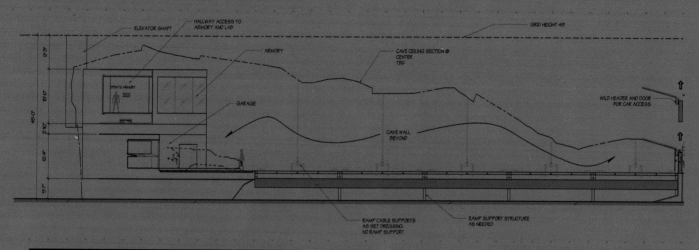

INT GARAGE SECTION ELEVATION NORTH - VIEW TOWARDS ARMORY

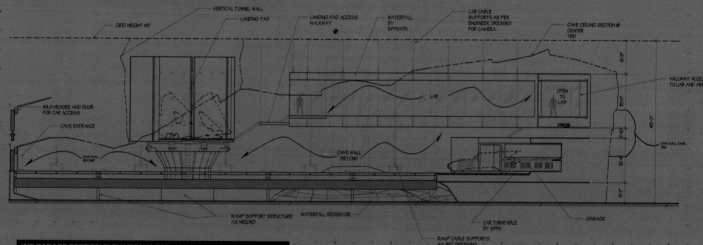

INT GARAGE SECTION ELEVATION SOUTH - VIEW TOWARDS LAB

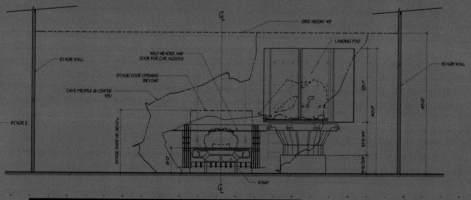

INT GARAGE SECTION ELEVATION WEST - VIEW TOWARDS GARAGE

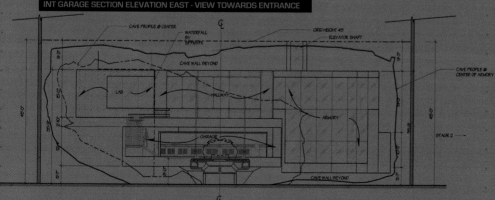

INT GARAGE SECTION ELEVATION EAST - VIEW TOWARDS ENTRANCE

NOTE:
WILD TUNNEL SECTION AND
REMOVABLE RAMP TO BE BUILT TO SUPPORT
FULL WEIGHT OF CAR IN MOTION AS PER
STUNTS AND TRANSPORTATION
REQUIREMENTS.
ALLOW FOR SECURING RAMP AND TUNNEL TO
STAGE FLOOR.

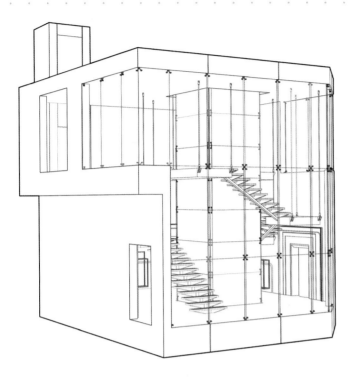

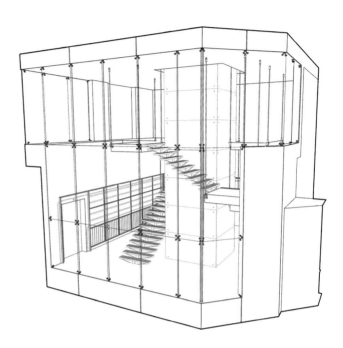

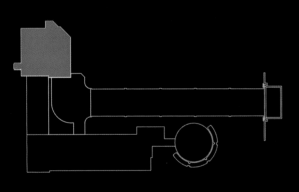

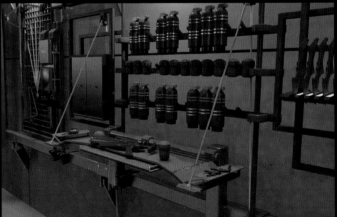

"The Batcave is often an opportunity for designers to create this gigantic, operatic space," Tatopoulos observes. "I wanted it to be different. Bruce basically had to adapt his architecture, his world, within that cave. It was not necessarily wide open and flat. The Batcave is an interpretation of his personality. It's a hard, bold look, there are no little stalagmites." The various areas built into the cave, such as the armory, are reached via staircases which all lack a certain feature. "I don't picture Batman needing railings," Tatopoulos reasons.

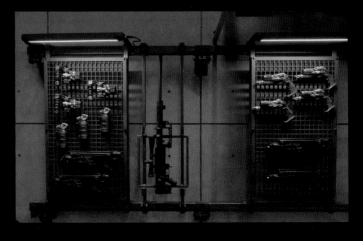

"ROBIN WAS AROUND
BEFORE HIS UNTIMELY DEMISE
AT THE HAND OF... THE CLUE'S
ON THE COSTUME!"

ZACK SNYDER

Alongside Batman's cutting-edge
tech, including the palm-activated
lock to access his suit, are
reminders of earlier days...

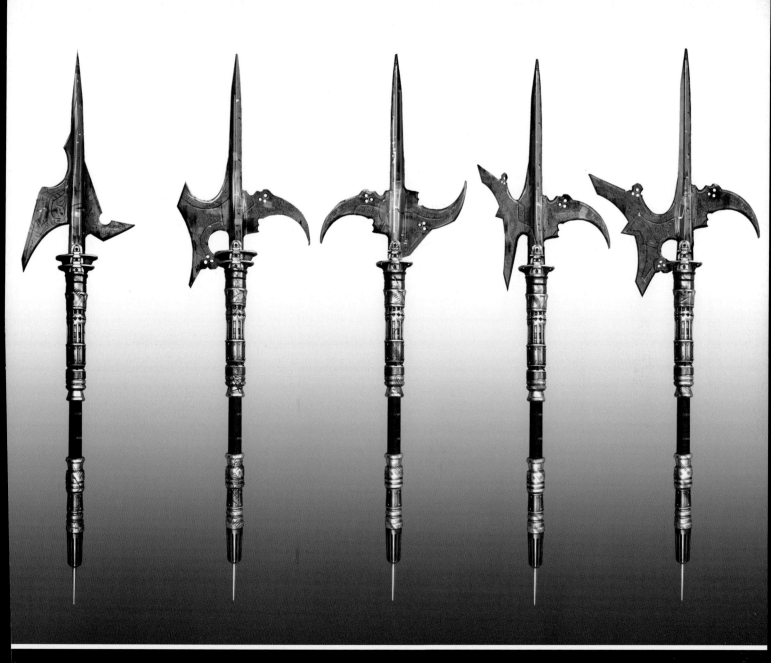

Robin's desecrated suit stands as a reminder for Batman of just what's at stake when he fails to get the better of the criminals he spends his life trying to bring to justice. This idea also fed through into Robin's weapon. Originally designed and constructed as a complete item, as filming drew closer the director decided to feature it as a broken artefact instead. "That was Zack saying 'look, maybe we should just make it look as if it's been broken and smashed,'" says props master Doug Harlocker. "So we deconstructed it in order to film it."

"The work station was attached to a gantry system so every one of those desks could be moved around," explains Tatopoulos. "The cables were attached to channels at the top of the room. So you could, at any moment, reconfigure the entire lab without dragging anything on the floor. About the only thing that is actually on the floor is his chair."

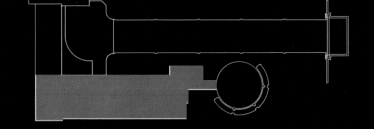

LABORATORY

The Batcave lab is also frequented by someone who's a lot more than just a butler to Bruce Wayne. "Alfred's his confidante, his sounding board, and most of all his tech guru," says co-producer Curt Kanemoto.

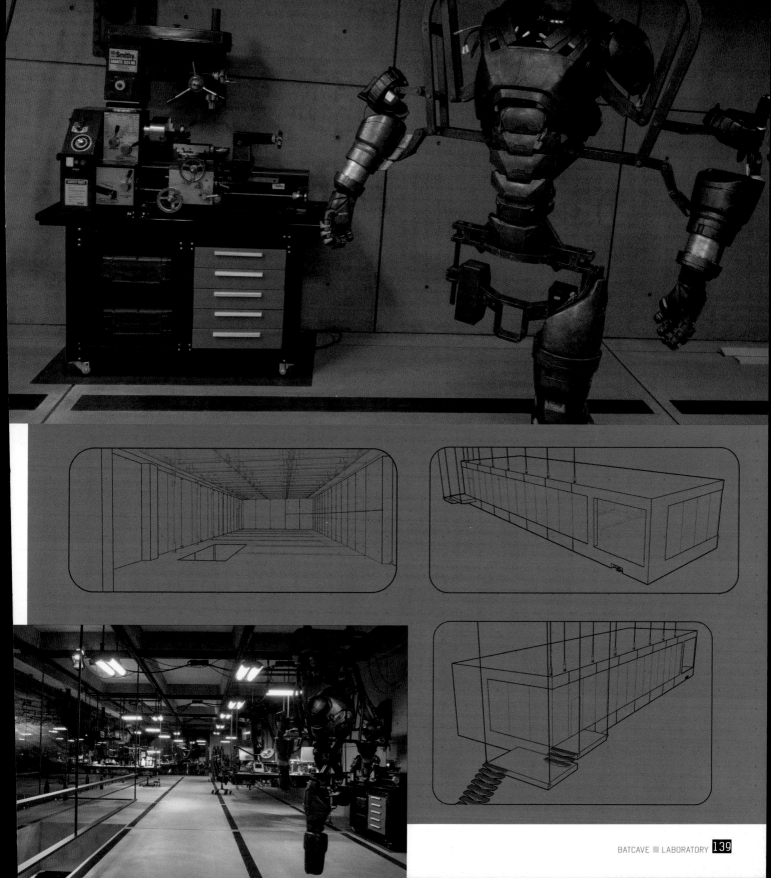

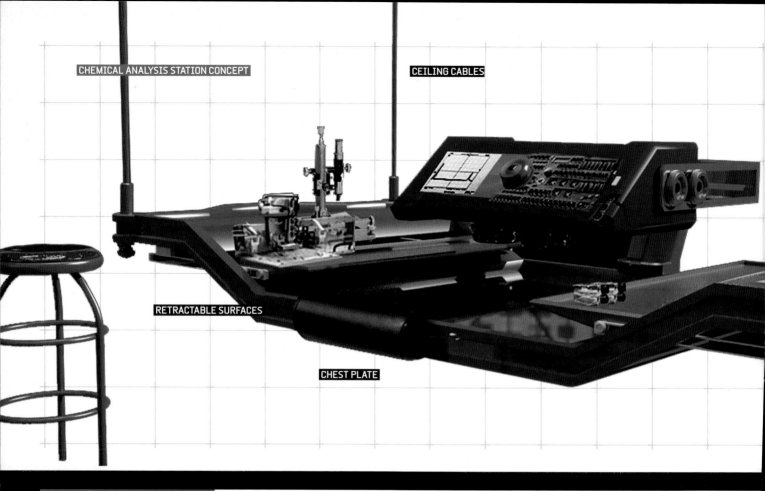

CHEMICAL ANALYSIS STATION CONCEPT

CEILING CABLES

RETRACTABLE SURFACES

CHEST PLATE

MONITOR DESK

UTILITY SINK

Designing a Batcave that can be easily adjusted as part of its function means it can cater to a director's requirements without extensive changes. "We're going to go back to that cave [in future films]," says Tatopoulos. "And that thing you thought you knew shows you more – without redesigning it."

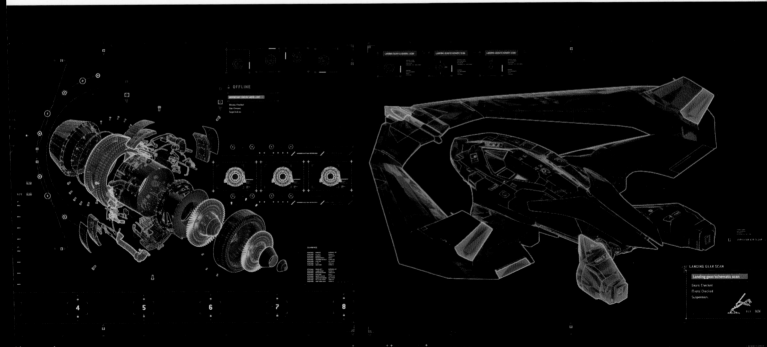

"I felt like it completes the look of the Batcave to have live graphics that work," Zack Snyder says, of the screen graphics that were actually practical elements of the set. "I know it seems fetishistic to have the graphics be particular to the Batcave, but we felt like that level of detail was within in the [capabilities] of Bruce Wayne and Alfred. And the only way not to be hacked is to use your own personal proprietary software and operating system."

"I WANTED THE BATCAVE TO BE ARCHITECTURALLY A REALLY MODERN DESIGN, A PRACTICAL WORKING SPACE."

ZACK SNYDER

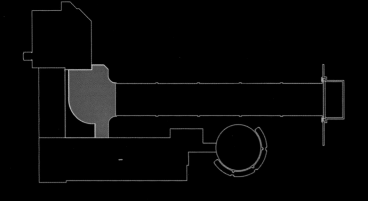

Having built the Batcave as an enclosed, roofed space, the crew had to find ways of lighting Tatopoulos's set. "Larry [Fong, Director of Photography] was challenged with those things right across the board and that's why he's such a great DP. I designed the whole thing so the cave was only lit by the inside light of the structures. There were no little lights here and there just to make pretty rocks. It gave me a chance to create a cave that goes from being lit almost like a lightbulb all the way to darkness by a slow process of not lighting the set any more. And that worked out really well."

GARAGE

Tatopoulos and concept artist Ed
Natividad chose charcoal and a deep,
orange-red as his signature colors for this
incarnation of Batman, Tatopoulos says,
"to steer away from the green that has
been used many times." It's particularly
in evidence in the garage area of the
Batcave, with its iconic turntable.

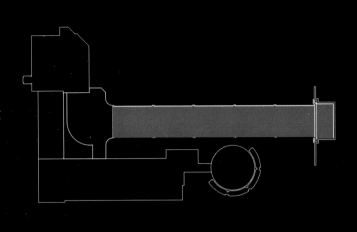

"It was Zack's idea that he wanted the Batmobile to come out of the lake," says Tatopoulos. "If you have the car coming out of the lake, you don't know what the origin of the Batcave is. You can't see it. A vehicle disappearing in water leaves no trace. So we had the concept that the last part of the tunnel is mechanical, that it lifts just at the edge of the water and the water drains off when the cage rises. The tunnel opens and the car can actually jump and land further into the forest so you don't have any tracks."

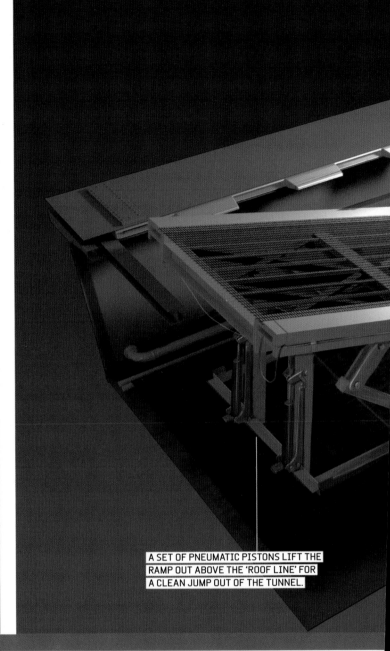

A SET OF PNEUMATIC PISTONS LIFT THE RAMP OUT ABOVE THE 'ROOF LINE' FOR A CLEAN JUMP OUT OF THE TUNNEL.

ACCESS TUNNEL

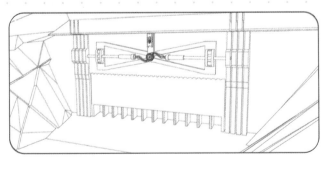

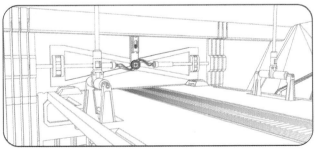

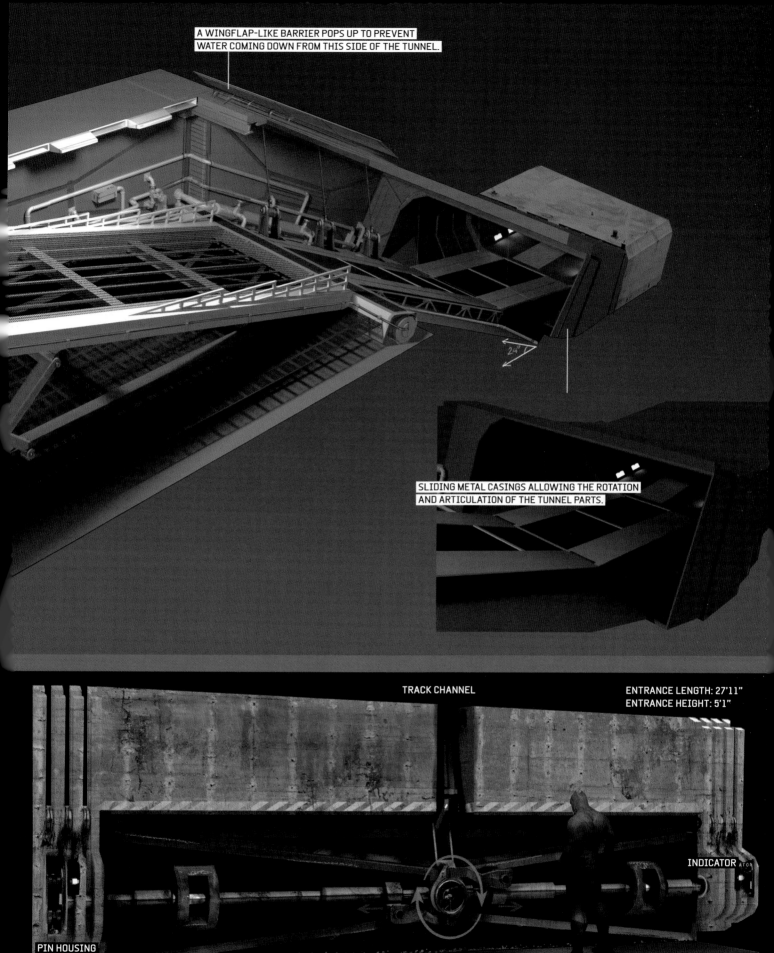

A WINGFLAP-LIKE BARRIER POPS UP TO PREVENT WATER COMING DOWN FROM THIS SIDE OF THE TUNNEL.

24°

SLIDING METAL CASINGS ALLOWING THE ROTATION AND ARTICULATION OF THE TUNNEL PARTS.

TRACK CHANNEL

ENTRANCE LENGTH: 27'11"
ENTRANCE HEIGHT: 5'1"

INDICATOR ATOR

PIN HOUSING

CLOCKWISE ROTATION SLIDES
PINS INTO LOCKED POSITION

"You could have a car that goes under water, but that's a little James Bond for me," says Tatopoulos. "We never want to be in sci-fi world with Batman. Whatever happens, Batman is a very real man and everything he has should feel very real."

"TO CONCEAL THE ENTRANCE TO THE BATCAVE, IT'S AN UNDERWATER ENTRANCE."
ZACK SNYDER

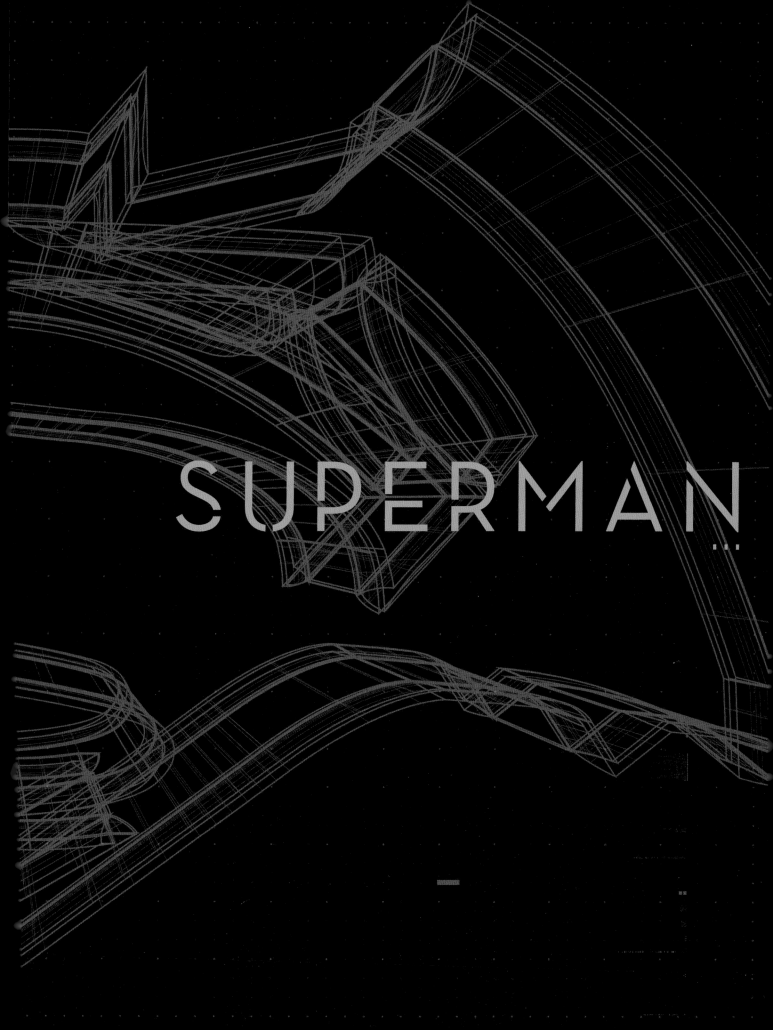

THE SUIT

Though the look of Superman's suit had already been established by costume designer Michael Wilkinson for *Man of Steel*, it still underwent a considerable evolution for *Batman v Superman: Dawn of Justice*. "Whenever we work on these Super Hero costumes, we do a whole lot of research and development in pre-production," explains Wilkinson. "We explore textiles and we think about what the suits are going to go through during the shoot. There's always very extensive stunt sequences and wirework and a very elaborate choreography that you have to think about that these costumes have to withstand. But there's also unusual things like going underwater and withstanding heavy rainfall, things like that. So we had a look at the fabrics underwater before we decided on colors and textures."

Stunt coordinator and second unit director Damon Caro consulted closely with Wilkinson about what he needed the costume to achieve: "He's such a pleasure to work with," says Caro. "Every time, we'll re-evaluate a suit or costume. From the last film, they improved Henry Cavill's costume immensely, as far as range of motion. They went back and revamped the entire suit. We're all on the same page, because at the end of the day the action is going to be better, the actor will move better, and the costume will look better if we're all working together."

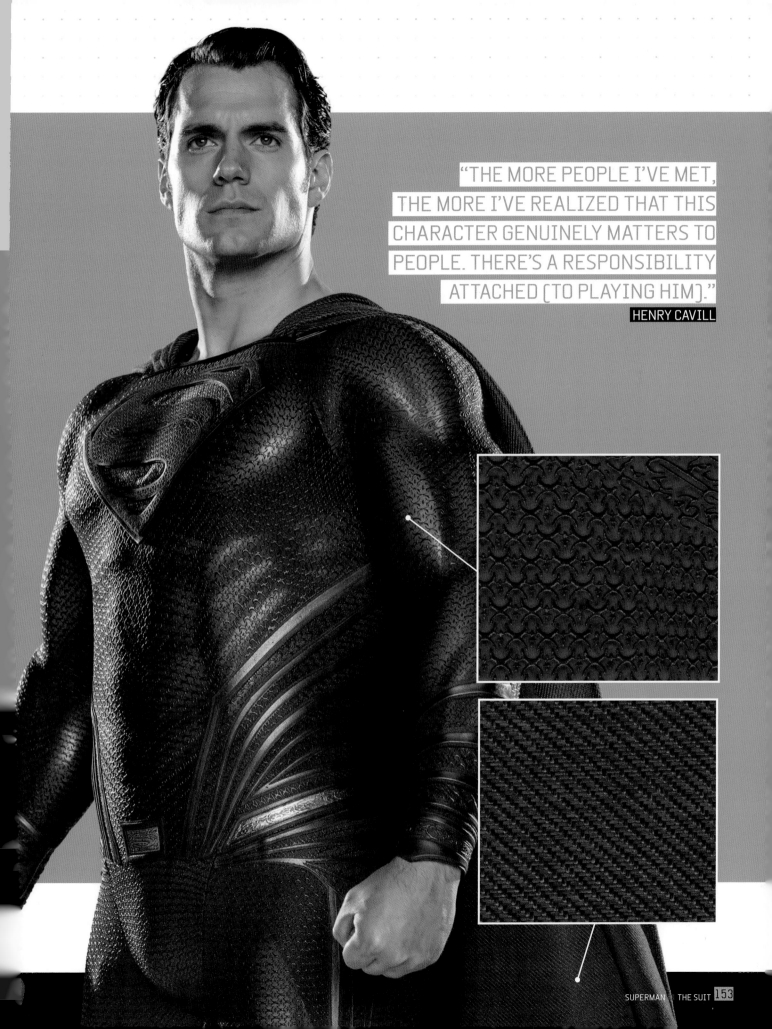

"THE MORE PEOPLE I'VE MET, THE MORE I'VE REALIZED THAT THIS CHARACTER GENUINELY MATTERS TO PEOPLE. THERE'S A RESPONSIBILITY ATTACHED [TO PLAYING HIM]."
HENRY CAVILL

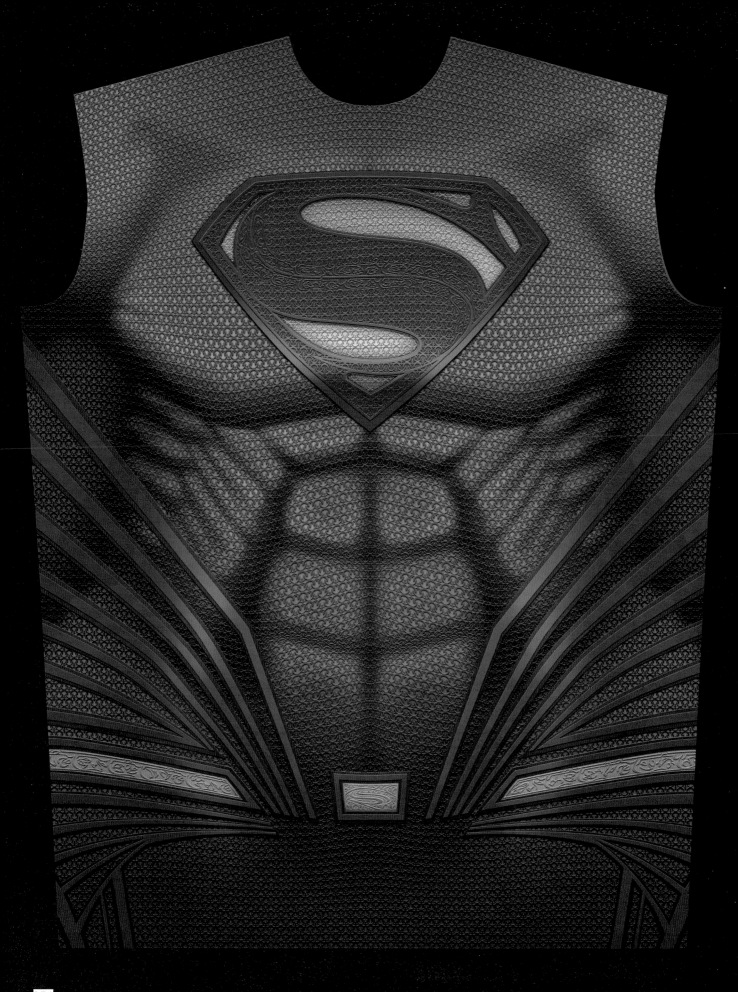

The production used the latest in costume technology – including digital printing – to realize the intricate details of Superman's suit.

Hidden in the embossing of Superman's suit is a quote from Joseph Campbell, who wrote what is acknowledged to be the most comprehensive work of comparative literature on the tradition of mythical heroes. "It's one of my favorite quotes and I feel like it applies to the hero's journey," says Zack Snyder. "That's the journey that Superman's on in our movie. Incorporating it now that we were well on the Superman road seemed appropriate." The quote, translated into Kryptonian by the scriptwriters, reads, "Where we had thought to be alone, we will be with all the world."

Superman's suit is as elegant, refined and pristine as Batman's is functional, brutal and battle-worn, providing a fitting contrast between the two heroes – one born and one self-made.

"SUPERMAN'S VIEW IS, GO ABOUT IT IN AN ETHICAL MANNER, WHEREAS BATMAN'S IS, INFLICT JUSTICE AT ANY COST. SO THAT'S WHERE THEY COME TO BLOWS – THEY'RE TRYING TO ACHIEVE THE SAME THING, BUT THROUGH ENTIRELY DIFFERENT METHODS."

HENRY CAVILL

KRYPTONITE CONTAINMENT SQUARE

TOP

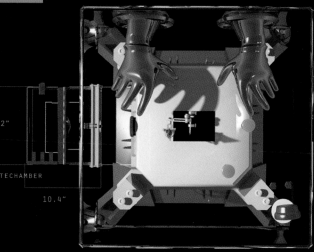

Gloves purchased from supplier

12"

Antechamber

10.4"

GLASS 3'
WIDE x 3' DEEP x 19.5" HIGH

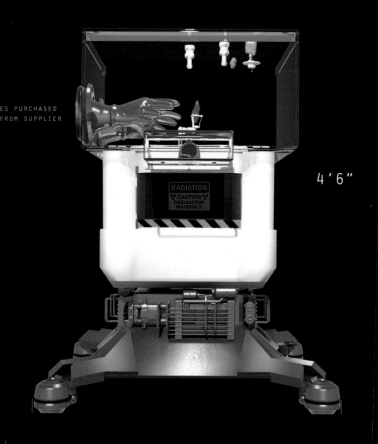

4'6"

RADIATION
CAUTION RADIOACTIVE MATERIALS

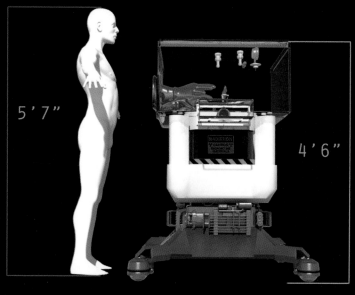

5'7"

4'6"

With both Lex Luthor (played by Jesse Eisenberg) and Batman seeking to destroy Superman, it was obvious that the film would need to feature some pretty heavy-duty kryptonite-related props. One of these is the containment module Luthor uses to house his store of the mineral. For Doug Harlocker and his team, it meant designing a prop that could be adapted mid-way through shooting. "The safe is in the base and there's hydraulics underneath that will lift up a piece of kryptonite," Harlocker explains. "So we made a tiny interface, a little plinth to hold a shard. The prop is glass and plexi and it's mechanical – we wired it so it could light up and it's on wheels so we could move it around."

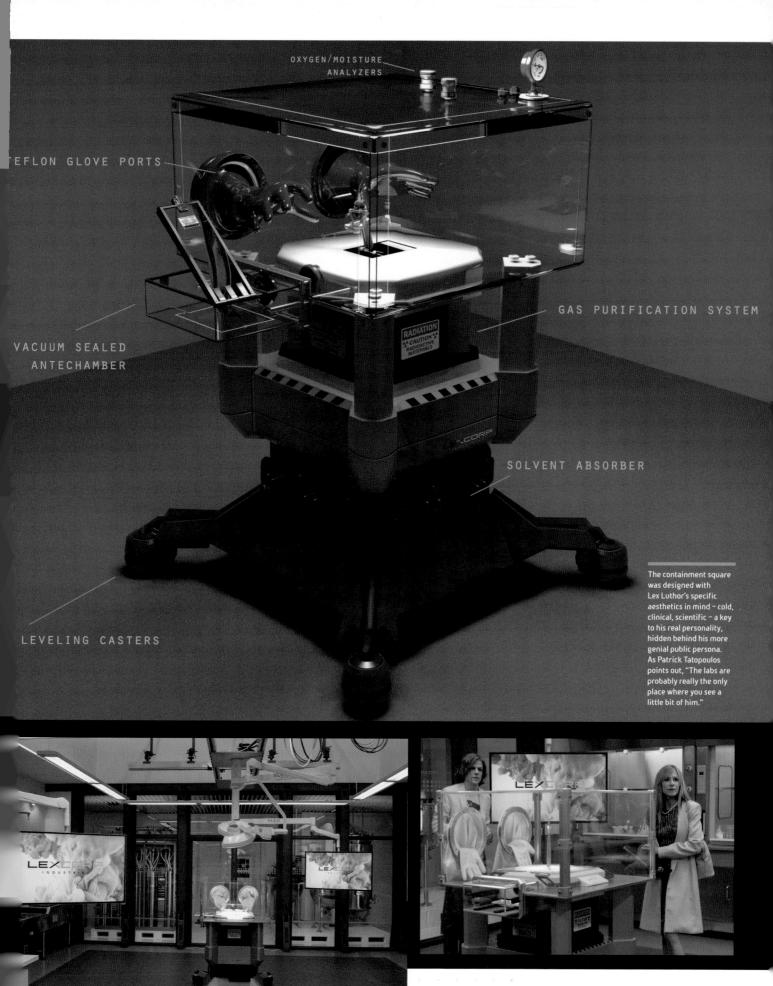

OXYGEN/MOISTURE
ANALYZERS

TEFLON GLOVE PORTS

VACUUM SEALED
ANTECHAMBER

RADIATION
CAUTION
RADIOACTIVE
MATERIALS

GAS PURIFICATION SYSTEM

SOLVENT ABSORBER

LEVELING CASTERS

The containment square
was designed with
Lex Luthor's specific
aesthetics in mind – cold,
clinical, scientific – a key
to his real personality,
hidden behind his more
genial public persona.
As Patrick Tatopoulos
points out, "The labs are
probably really the only
place where you see a
little bit of him."

MICROFLUIDIC TISSUE TRANSPORTER

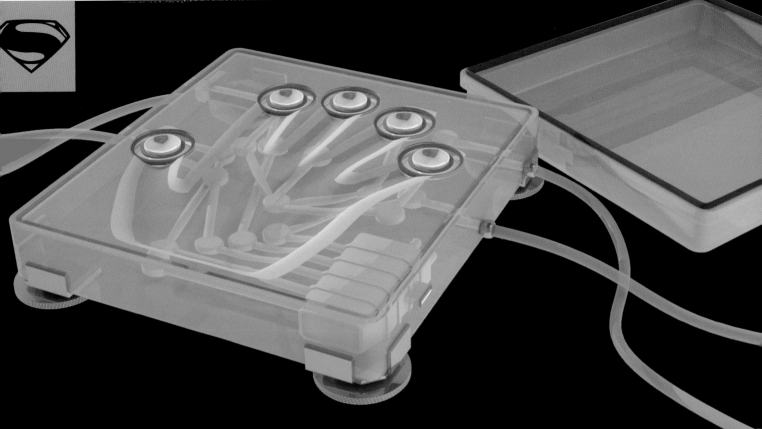

"The mandate for this machine was hard," Harlocker laughs. "Zack's like, 'Yeah, he takes (another character's) fingerprints and he puts them in this thing and then later on he takes his own hand and he touches them. They attach to his fingers and he puts his fingers up to the vessel and that allows him access.' And so it had to be small enough and technical enough. In real science right now there are these machines, hydrators to keep tissue alive. So we made it based a little bit on science and we took it up a notch. "

The make-up department produced skin-like appliances to stand in for the excised fingerprints, which were then placed in the prop and coated with glycerine so that when the actor touched his own fingers to them, they would adhere to his fingertips. Visual Effects then blended the process in post-production.

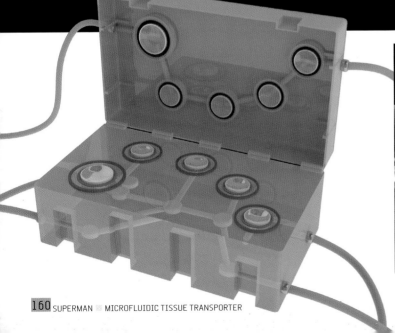

SCOUT SHIP

When it came to building the interiors of the ship, Tatopoulos was careful to build on the aesthetic established in Man of Steel. "You want to make sure that the audience can recognize where it's come from, that they can remember that space."

Returning to the Kryptonian scout ship first seen in Man of Steel allowed the production to change the look of it a little. "The thing that's cool is that we don't even really need to contrast Kryptonian tech with modern human tech because the design school that we chose for Krypton is kind of a closed circle," says Snyder. "Whatever you put it next to it feels foreign." Nevertheless, Tatopoulos took the opportunity to introduce some new aspects to the ship. "It crashed in Man of Steel, so I came up with the idea that maybe there was some acid inside the craft that burned the corridors. It gave us the chance to use the same aesthetic but give it a different texture."

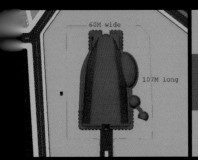
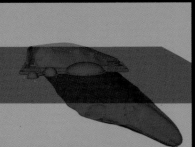
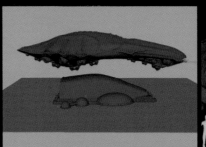
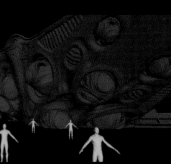

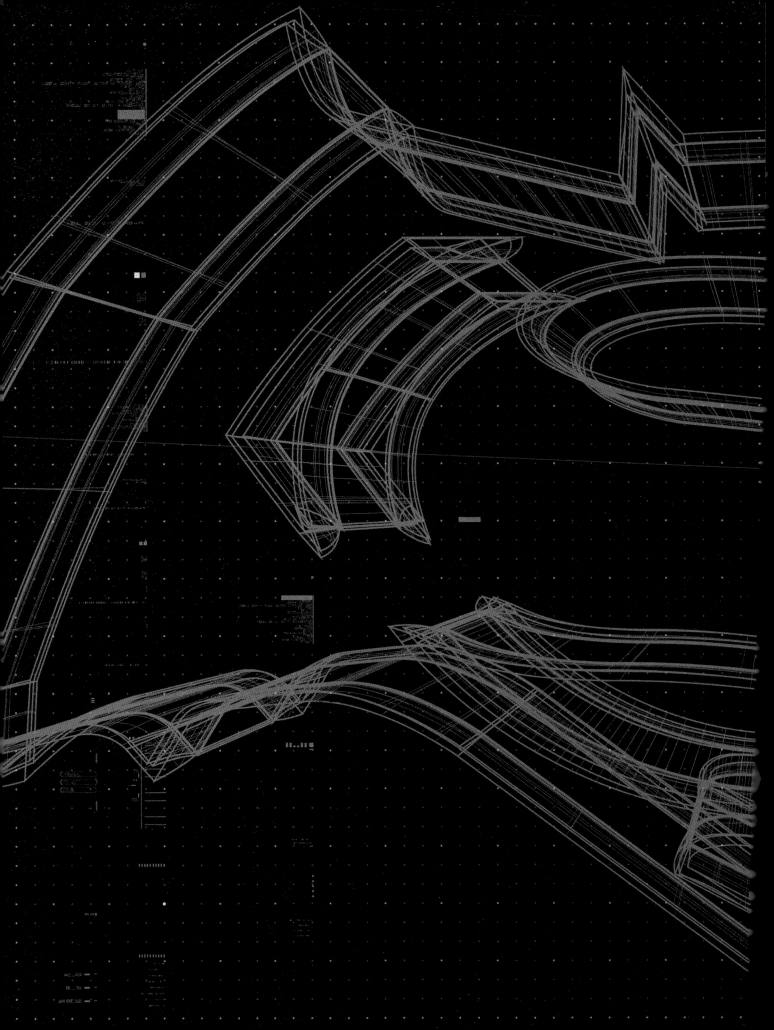

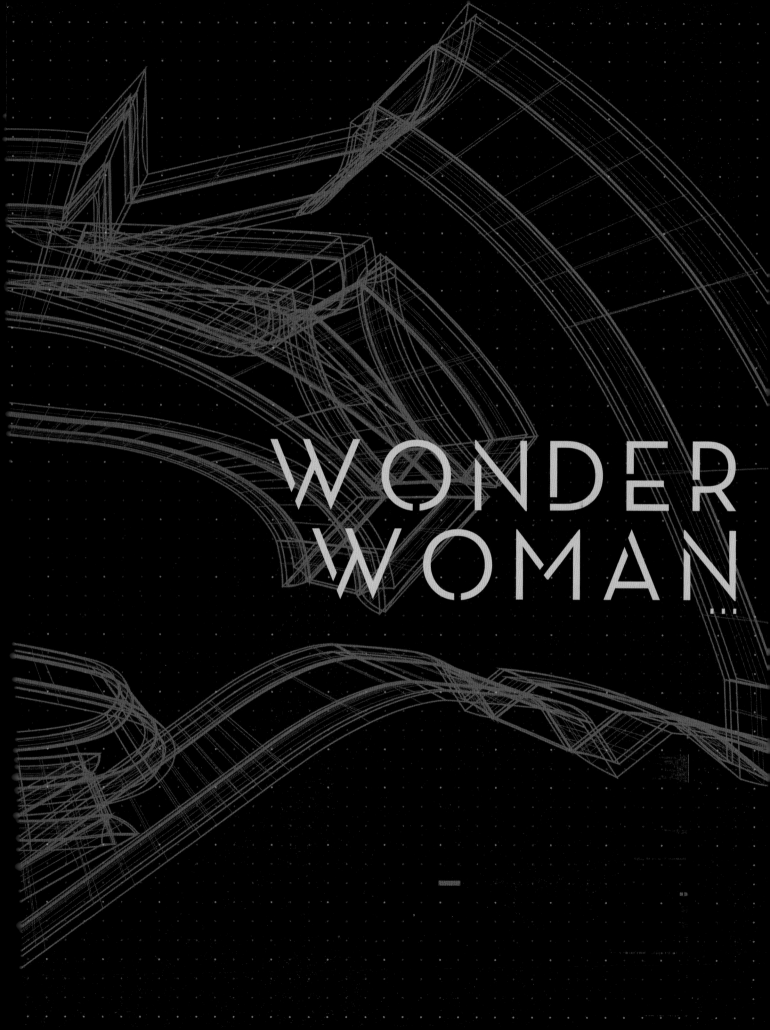

ARMOR

"We really wanted the character to have power and a sense of intimidation, but also balance that with grace and majesty," says costume designer Michael Wilkinson, of the film's approach to Wonder Woman, played by Gal Gadot. One way in which the production imbued these qualities was in the attention to detail invested in the character's armor. "One of the first things that Zack and I talked about is, she's been wearing this costume for her entire history, which is 3,000 years," Wilkinson points out. "It's never changed. You can see the history of the character within the costume itself."

Wilkinson drew influences from ancient Greek gladiators and warriors to find the shape of Wonder Woman's costume, embellishing it with the wear and tear of centuries of battles from sword nicks to bullet holes.

"THE COSTUME IS VERY MUCH INSPIRED BY AND A TRIBUTE TO THE ORIGINAL DESIGNS FOR WONDER WOMAN."

ZACK SNYDER

LASSO

To realise Wonder Woman's iconic lasso, Wilkinson turned to Doug Harlocker. "That was a tricky thing," the prop master admits. "We didn't just want it to look like a piece of cable. So we found a specific braid and showed Zack a variety of scales, and we decided that a length of twenty feet, when wrapped, looked appropriate on her body. We made it gold and gave it a level of distress and made a quick-release for her belting so that she could just whip it off and hold it. Then we put a fiber optic cable into it so that we could have some interactive lighting – visual effects used that as reference and enhanced it."

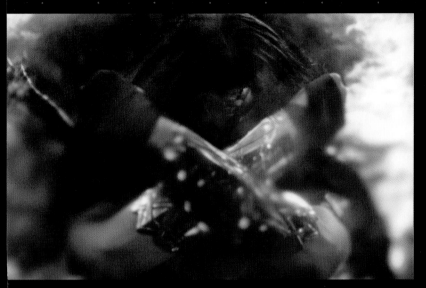

Another aspect of retaining elements of Wonder Woman's original costume can be seen in her metal arm enclosures. More than simply additions to her armor, the bracelets are capable of both absorbing energy and deflecting incoming artillery. Together with the rest of her costume, they complete the idea that the character has taken on a very light and flexible yet practical suit of armor. "It feels like something she could actually fight in," points out Deborah Snyder. "I think it's gorgeous."

BRACELETS

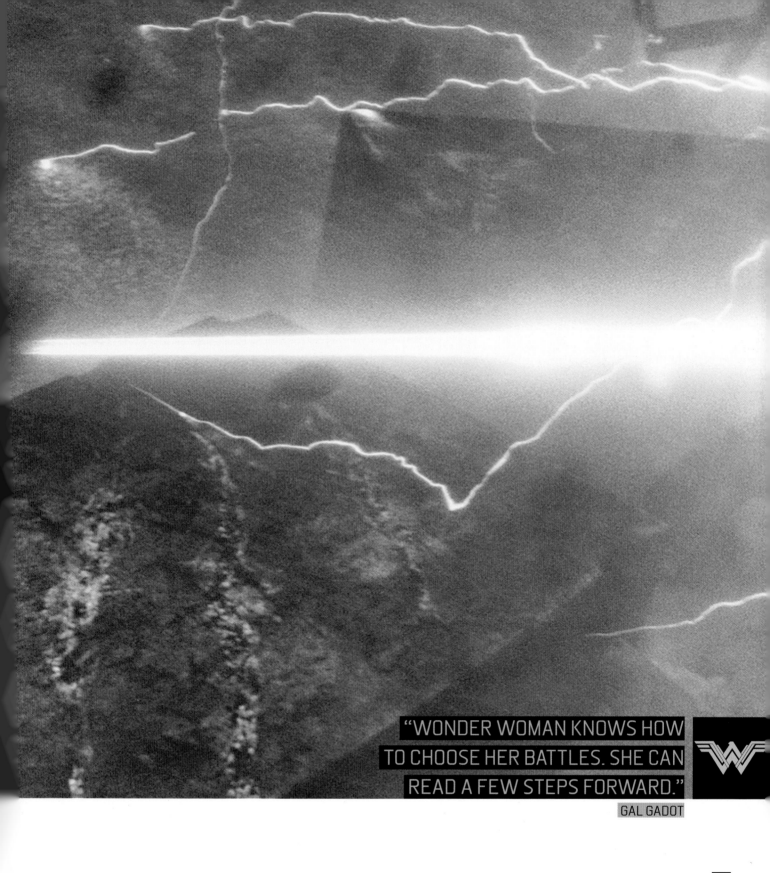

"WONDER WOMAN KNOWS HOW TO CHOOSE HER BATTLES. SHE CAN READ A FEW STEPS FORWARD."

GAL GADOT

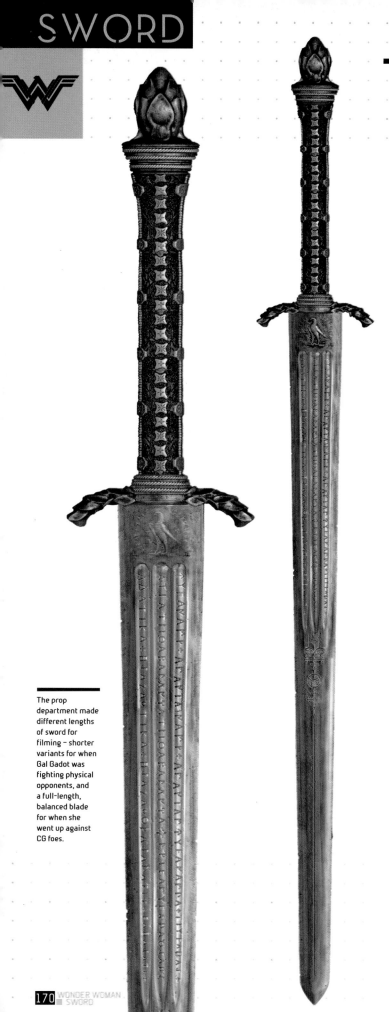

The prop department made different lengths of sword for filming – shorter variants for when Gal Gadot was fighting physical opponents, and a full-length, balanced blade for when she went up against CG foes.

"We were trying to figure out how to make a really graceful sword for Wonder Woman," says Harlocker. "Zack wanted some inscription on both her shield and her sword, so we needed to create a language. We talked to a linguist who specialises in ancient scripts and extinct languages. There's a Joseph Campbell quote in his book *Goddesses: Mystery of the Feminine Divine* that Zack really liked. So we translated that into this kind of hybrid extinct language and engraved it onto the blades, and around the outside of the shield."

The translated Joseph Campbell quote engraved on Wonder Woman's sword reads, "Life is killing life all the time and so the goddess kills herself in the sacrifice of her own animal."

SHIELD

Doug Harlocker and his team spent a long time finding the right way to age Wonder Woman's shield. "It's all about the paint," he says. "We found a really beautiful texture, almost like an oil painting. I wanted it to feel like that eagle at one point was much more pronounced and over the years it had faded into the background. It really started to feel like an oil painting on the front, but made out of some unearthly material, and the gold leaf made it look old but not tawdry."

Harlocker explains that the shield and sword took a lot of work. "They were really tricky props to make. They're establishing a character and a franchise and we all took it extremely seriously."

"I'M VERY PROUD OF THE SHIELD."

DOUG HARLOCKER

One of the biggest challenges for Michael Wilkinson was to create an armored costume that would still provide ease of movement for Gal Gadot during filming. After all, metal isn't known for its flexible properties. The solution involved the costume department developing its own textile that would behave as required. "We actually developed a material that looked like metal, was able to take a paint finish and had a beautiful ancient feel to it that was, in fact, flexible," says Wilkinson. "I designed the breastplate to be sectioned. It has expansion joints so she's able to breathe and to bend and to do all of her amazing stunt moves as well as look like she's encased in this incredibly strong metal armor."

"We wanted to really respect and honor the original designs for Wonder Woman and keep the iconography that people are used to alive," Zack Snyder concludes.

"WHEN I SAW ONE OF THE PLAYBACKS ON THE FIRST DAY THAT WE SHOT THE THREE OF US TOGETHER, I NEEDED TO PINCH MYSELF. IT'S SO STRONG."
GAL GADOT

ACKNOWLEDGMENTS

Titan Books would like to thank all involved for their hard work in making this book possible. Thank you to the authors, Adam Newell and Sharon Gosling, for their passion and expertise in bringing this book together.

Special thanks go to the filmmakers for creating such a wonderful movie and to those involved in creating this Tech Manual. In particular Wes Coller, Curt Kanemoto, Spencer Douglas, Shane Thompson, Alisha Stevens, Adam Forman, Elaine Piechowski, Josh Anderson, Nik Primack, Patrick Tatopoulos, Doug Harlocker, Charles Roven, and Zack and Deborah Snyder.

The filmmakers wish to extend their thanks to the crew who made the movie, including but not limited to: Warren Manser, Jay Olivia, Jared Purrington, Michael Meyers, Vance Kovacs, Victor Martinez, Robert McKinnon, Christian Scheurer, Ed Natividad, Tim Earls, Charles Roven, Deborah Snyder, Chris Terrio, Wesley Coller, Geoff Johns, David S. Goyer, Bob Kane, Bill Finger, Jerry Siegel, Joe Shuster, Steve Mnuchin, Christopher Nolan, Emma Thomas, Benjamin Melniker, Michael E. Uslan, Gregor Wilson, Jim Rowe, Curt Kanemoto, Bruce Moriarity, Misha Bukowski, Damon Caro, David W. Paris, David Nowell, Scott Hecker, Chris Jenkins, Michael Keller, Tim Rigby, Andrea Wertheim, Trevor J.W. Christie, Troy Sizemore, Lorin Flemming, Beat Frutiger, Greg Hooper, Kevin Ishioka, Tom Frohling, Tom Castronovo, Justin Lang, Shari Ratliff, Carolyn Loucks, John Clothier, William Dalgleish, Mark Twight, Michael Blevins, David Brenner, Josh Jaggers, Tricia Mulgrew, Lora Kennedy, Kristy Carlson, Chuck Michael, Margit Pfeiffer, Zahida Bacchus, Kimi Webber, Michael McGee, Gladys Tong, Bob Morgan, Jennifer Jobst, Jr Hawbaker, Stephanie Porter, Victoria Down, Kristin Berge, Jim Grce, Gary Dodd, Kevin Erb, Eric Matthies, Mitchell Rubinstein, Erick Donaldson, Larry Hubs, Robert Johnson, Bria Kinter, Jeff Markwith, Anshuman Prasad, Richard Reynolds, Scott Schneider, Tony Bohorquez, Jeff Frost, Joe Hiura, Kelly Rae Hemenway, Jason Sweers, Deborah Jurvis, Allison Klein, Chris Strother, Joel Whist, Arnand Kularajah, Brady Endres, Adam Forman, Alisha Stevens, Celeste Coller, Jackie Levine, Joanne Lazarus Grobe, Eric Wolf, Madison Weireter, Nicholas Boak, Bradley Elliot, Bradley Good, Kevin McClo, Michael Papac, Jonas Kirk, Bryan Holloway, Frank Piercy, Carmine Goglia, Eric Rhodes, Lee Rhadigan, Michael Scot Risley, Scott Denis, Brent Godek, Scott Grace, Jonathan Miller, Patrick Velasquez, Bobby Griffon, Lee Anne Muldoon, Hans Zimmer, Junkie XI, Stefan Sonnenfeld, Guillaume Rocheron, David P.I. James, Harry Mukhopadhyay, Keith F. Miller, Joe Letteri, Kyle Robinson, Bryan Hirota, Julie Orosz, Ben Breckenridge, Paul Becker, Chad Cortvriendt, Company 3, Mpc, Scanline, Weta Digital Limited, Double Negative, Method Studios, Shade, Perception, Panic, Mova, Mocap Design, Gentle Giant Studios, Gardiner Consulting, 4dmax, Pictorvision, Gener8, Teamworks Digital, The Resistance Vfx, Shane Thompson, Spencer Douglas, Josh Anderson.

The filmmakers would also like to thank the team at Titan Books for all their hard work - Beth Lewis, Simon Ward, Amazing 15, Nick Landau, and Vivian Cheung.

AUTHOR BIOS

Adam Newell is an editor and writer who has been involved with putting together many film and TV-related titles over the years, including *Firefly: A Celebration* and *Prometheus: The Art of the Film*.

A fan of all things fantasy, horror and sci-fi, Sharon Gosling is a UK-based writer of both non-fiction and fiction, as well as working as a pop-culture magazine editor and audio drama producer.

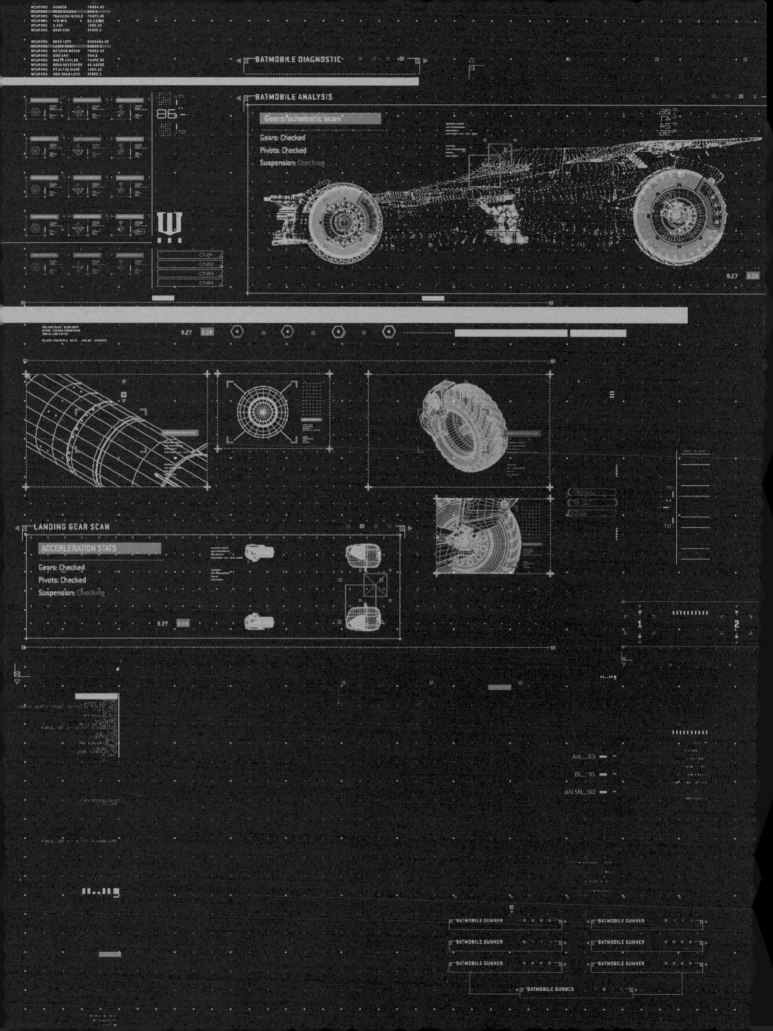